small-group teaching

small-group teaching

Shlomo Sharan
Tel-Aviv University

Yael Sharan
Kibbutz Teachers College,
Tel-Aviv

Educational Technology Publications
Englewood Cliffs, New Jersey 07632

Library of Congress Cataloging in Publication Data

Sharan, Shlomo, 1932-
  Small-group teaching.

  Bibliography: p.
  Includes index.
  1. Group work in education. 2. Role playing.
3. Simulated environment (Teaching method) I. Sharan,
Yael, joint author. II. Title.
LB1032.S4513   371.3   75-42019
ISBN 0-87778-091-9

Adapted and translated by the authors from a book of the same title, in the Hebrew language, by Shlomo Sharan and Yael Sharan, first edition published in 1974, second revised edition published in 1975 by Schocken Publishing Company, Tel-Aviv, Israel.

Printed in the United States of America.

Library of Congress Catalog Card Number:
75-42019.

International Standard Book Number:
0-87778-091-9.

First Printing: February, 1976.

For Our Parents

Acknowledgments

The authors wish to thank the following publishers and authors for granting their permission to reproduce selections or publish adaptations from their books:

The series of lessons, Developing Skills for Participation in Small Groups, appearing on pages 65-71 of this book, is adapted from a booklet entitled *They Help Each Other*, by J. Baker, T. Smith, B. Walters, and R. Wetzel, published in 1971 by the San Bernardino County Schools, San Bernardino, California. The publication was supported by the U.S. Office of Education, Bilingual Education Program. The Exercise for Developing Listening Skills, on pages 71-72, and the Exercise in Cooperative Planning, pages 81-84, are adapted from A. Gorman's book, *Teachers and Learners: The Interactive Process of Education*, published by Allyn and Bacon, Inc., Boston, Massachusetts, 1969. The game for promoting participation in a discussion, appearing on page 109, is reproduced by permission from *Learning Discussion Skills Through Games*, pages 32-33, by Gene Stanford and Barbara Dodds Stanford, Copyright © 1969 by Scholastic Magazines, Inc., published by Citation Press, a division of Scholastic Magazines, Inc. On pages 111-112 of this book is the "Murder Mystery" game reprinted by permission of Prentice-Hall, Inc., from *Joining Together: Group Theory and Group Skills*, by David W. and Frank P. Johnson, Copyright © 1975 by Prentice-Hall, Inc., Englewood Cliffs, New Jersey. The observation sheets

Foreword

Although many teachers would like to experiment with work in small-group settings, they are unlikely to do so. They typically receive no training specific to this area; and when they try it out for themselves the results are often distressing. The educational value of the group interaction is doubtful; the students do not spontaneously cooperate with one another; and frequently one person dominates the interaction while the others become dissatisfied with the activity and withdraw from the group. Small-group activity, if it is to meet the educational and social goals of the teacher, must be structured carefully; there are specific skills which must be learned by the student for sustained small-group interaction; activity must often be highly structured through sophisticated planning.

The Sharans have combed the literature inside and outside the conventional field of professional education. They have come up with a wide variety of techniques which will solve the technical problems we have just described. Furthermore, they present these techniques in such a way that a teacher with no special training or access to classroom consultants or expensive curriculum materials may use these techniques in an ordinary classroom. Yael Sharan, a highly experienced specialist in teaching, has worked with Shlomo Sharan, a social psychologist, to insure that each technique described includes a discussion of just what the teacher's role should be in planning, carrying out, and guiding these activities.

There are many excellent concrete examples for the teacher who wants to begin using small-group techniques.

At first glance these techniques, ranging from classroom research groups to role playing and simulation, appear to be selected on an eclectic basis. The introductory chapters, however, reveal a consistent educational philosophy which underlies the choice of techniques for this book.

The Sharans have two major concerns for the experience of children in classrooms. The first stems from their rejection of the child's role as a passive learner, under the complete domination of the teacher's leadership. They want to increase the child's sense of efficacy by teaching him to control more of his own opportunities for learning. They do not accomplish this goal by allowing the student total autonomy as in many of the open classrooms, now so popular. Instead, the child achieves control over his environment through learning to plan and carry out activities as a group member. The art of group planning and productive group interaction is not left to chance. Included in this book are criteria to be used by the students themselves to judge the quality of their own group process. Through easy stages, groups learn to achieve a high degree of effectiveness in selecting workable goals and carrying them out on their own. These criteria for group process are presented in such a way that they can be adapted for the youngest to the adult student in the small-group setting. These techniques are particularly useful for students without previous opportunities for group learning.

The second major concern in selecting these techniques is a rationale developed from the point of view of Dewey and Piaget. The Sharans argue that more active learning which organizes and assimilates experience through interaction with the environment will help to develop logical thought and higher order verbal communication skills. Furthermore, this kind of active participation will decrease the sense of competition and anxiety which is often associated with schooling, and will increase the atmosphere of cooperation and personal gratification.

In the techniques suggested, neither the quality of the interpersonal processes nor the intellectual calibre of the group's activities is left to chance. Among the techniques used to assure that the experience is an educational one are the specific assignment of rotated roles such as group leader, the use of rules of a game for the group, exercises to increase listening skills, lists of criteria for group self-evaluation, specific norms for the development of an independent group planning process, and techniques to increase the' sense of efficacy and cohesiveness of the group. Use of a number of these techniques should produce classroom groups capable of independent functioning and quite successful in achieving their own intellectual goals. In addition, group members should learn what each person has to offer in a way calculated to reduce stereotypical views students hold of one another in conventional classrooms.

This book was originally written to meet the need of teachers in Israel for the introduction of groupwork in their classrooms without expensive materials; their large classes and lack of formal preparation for this kind of teaching had to be considered as well. When Dr. Sharan was a Visiting Fellow at the Stanford University School of Education, my seminar of experienced educators worked with him trying to find models of skilled groupwork practice for him to observe among local teachers. Much to our surprise, we discovered that very few teachers in the San Francisco Bay Area were carrying on groupwork of any sophistication. They too lacked ready access to useful techniques. It became clear that there was just as much of a need for the book here in the United States as there was in Israel.

Dr. Sharan, with characteristic scholarly zeal, has combed the literature for workable ideas. Sharan's unique background as a clinical psychologist, social researcher, and educator allows him to evaluate the effectiveness of these procedures in achieving his underlying goals for the classroom. Yael Sharan has contributed her clear understanding of what it takes to make more abstract and theoretical ideas workable and practicable for teachers who may have no access to help other than this volume. The Sharans have culled the best from all sources and have presented it in a form to meet the needs of the advanced or beginning professional who wishes to explore and experiment with active learning and improved classroom interaction.

Elizabeth G. Cohen
Stanford University

November, 1975

Preface

Small-group teaching comprises a wide range of techniques for structuring the relationship between students, and as such it is not a teaching method. Rather, it includes a variety of approaches which create social contexts conducive to cooperative learning. These different techniques can be used, as the need arises, in sequence, in conjunction with each other, or integrated with other methods, such as forms of individualized teaching, open classroom, or large-group teaching. Moreover, various types of strategies can be used simultaneously in the same classroom, including different forms of small groups. Indeed, current thinking about open education (Barth, 1972; Stephens, 1974) and individualized instruction (Bishop, 1971), for example, emphasizes the importance of small-group learning in promoting cooperation and collective investigation in the classroom.

While the versatile nature of small-group teaching facilitates its use with many forms of classroom instruction, the small-group approach certainly can be employed as the prevailing set of techniques, with other approaches used as complementary methods. The authors' bias is squarely in favor of using cooperative small groups as the preferred instructional strategy for encouraging student involvement in learning within a social context (Johnson and Johnson, 1974).

Small-group techniques are also applicable in a variety of organizational settings. Team teaching, the multi-unit school, the non-graded school, or continuous-progress instruction ultimately must all create conditions for students to relate to each other during the learning process. Small-group techniques can help teachers to make these relationships productive and gratifying for all participants.

In light of the wide range of organizational and instructional settings which can accommodate small-group teaching, it is impossible to formulate *a priori* rules for determining the amount of classroom time to be devoted to small-group activities or other forms of instruction. The allocation of time blocks to any given instructional technique will vary from one classroom to another, and from one day to the next in the same classroom. Time schedules will be set according to student interest and skill, the topic being investigated, and the teacher's preferences and style.

Although this book was written originally in the Hebrew language, for Israeli teachers, it is an "American" book in more ways than one. Firstly, it is based exclusively on current literature in the United States. Secondly, it was written while the first author was a Special Research Fellow of the National Institute of Mental Health at the School of Education, Stanford University, and later a Visiting Professor, Department of Psychology, California State University at San Diego. Sincere thanks go to these institutions for the opportunity they provided for study, observation in schools, and time to devote to writing.

We wish to express our deepest gratitude to Marian Shai, who read the entire manuscript and skillfully made it more readable. Thanks too go to Sadie Gottlieb and to Judy Gottlieb for their devoted assistance in typing the manuscript. We greatly appreciate Sadie Gottlieb's careful reading of the proofs.

Shlomo Sharan, Yael Sharan
Ramat Aviv, ISRAEL
Tishri, 5736
September, 1975

Table of Contents

Acknowledgments vii
Foreword by Elizabeth G. Cohen... ix
Preface xiii

Chapter One. Why Small Groups 3
    Values and Assumptions 3
    What Is a Group? 5
    Advantages of Small Groups.. 7
    Small-Group Learning and Academic Achievement........ 10
    Teacher and Student Roles 15
    The Promise and Problems of Small-Group Teach-
    ing 16

Chapter Two. How Small Groups Work 21
    Social Relations 22
    Communication 28
    Selection of Members and Tasks 32
    Group Leadership.. 37
    Group Development... 43

Chapter Three. Types of Small Groups.................................. 47
    The Research Group.. 47
    The Discussion Group 52
    Learning Centers 53

Learning Through Group Play 54
Combining Different Kinds of Groups for Learning........ 57

Chapter Four. Organizing Small Group Learning 61
TRANSITION 61
Initial Steps for Subdividing Classes.............................. 61
Buzz Groups 63
Developing Skills for Participation in Small Groups 65
Exercise for Developing Listening Skills 71
Teaching Reading in Groups 73
COOPERATIVE PLANNING 75
A Small-Group Approach to Unit Teaching 77
Studying the Environment: An Example 88

Chapter Five. Group Discussion 97
Clear Planning 98
Effective Discussion Leadership 105
Total and Constructive Participation 114
Evaluation of Discussion and Outcome 115

Chapter Six. Activity Centers and Learning Centers 127
Activity Centers: Introduction...................................... 128
Learning Centers: Introduction 128
ACTIVITY CENTERS 129
Curriculum in the Open Classroom 129
Activity Cards 136
How to Begin 136
LEARNING CENTERS 140
Types of Centers 141
Designing Learning Centers 148
Components of a Center 149
How to Begin 152
Changing the Centers 153
Record-keeping and Evaluation 154

Recording Students' Choice of Stations 154
Recording Skills 155
Evaluating the Centers 155
Evaluating Adjustment to the Centers 156
Individual Consultations 157
Guidelines for Selecting Materials 157

Chapter Seven. Role Playing 159
Introduction 159
Some Implications of Role Playing 161
When to Use Role Playing 165
Criteria for the Use of Role Playing 169
Steps in Preparing for Role Playing 170
Guiding the Play 178
Becoming Accustomed to Role Playing 180
Role Play in the Context of Small-Group Teaching........ 182
A New Student in Class: Exploring Ethnic Rela-
tions Through Role Playing 183

Chapter Eight. Simulation Games 187
Introduction 187
Some Specific Qualities of Simulation Games 192
The Virtues of Planning Your Own Games 198
Role Playing and Simulation Games............................ 200
Designing a Simulation Game 201
Observations About Simulation Gaming 212
A Simulation Game: "Negotiations" 213

Postscript to Teaching Staffs 217

References 219

Index 233

About the Authors 237

small-group teaching

Chapter One

Why Small Groups

Values and Assumptions

Every approach to teaching is based upon a set of values and assumptions about the psychology of children's learning, about how children and teachers should conduct themselves in school, about the goals of education. These values have a strong influence on teachers' professional behavior. The values of small-group teaching, as presented in this book, are derived largely from the philosophical outlook of John Dewey, and the psychology of Jean Piaget. Let us state some fundamental principles which characterize this approach.

Educational planning and practice should be primarily child-centered; this means that the students' own interests and abilities should be the point of departure for planning their educational experiences. In fact, children should be active in planning their learning experiences as well as in performing learning tasks. Children of all ages, at least through high school, learn best and enjoy it more when they learn ideas and concepts directly through activities instead of merely being receivers of verbal knowledge. It is better for them to *practice* many of the disciplines they study than simply to learn *about* them. Many topics and methods of learning become personally relevant to students when they engage in the actual process of investigation typical of a particular discipline or profession. Students can be intellectually stimulated by history, city planning, or law enforcement if the learning method is realistic and bears relation to real life.

Learning is facilitated by activating the student; and learning relevant to intellectual development takes place as a result of a dynamic interaction between the child and his environment: he must organize and assimilate new experiences into the store of concepts he already possesses. Environmental events are understood in light of our intellectual background and level of development. They do not have a specific meaning simply because the adults presenting them to the child think they have that meaning. One of the major assumptions of small-group teaching is that we are most likely to increase the child's chances of gratification from his learning experiences by maximizing his role in planning and carrying out the learning tasks. Too much of traditional school teaching is in rote fashion and bears little meaning for the students.

Another central educational concept contributed by the Dewey-Piaget school is that the student's active role in learning is best fostered in a social context. Students should be encouraged, by the very structure of the learning situation, to develop cooperative relations with their classmates. Learning is more pleasurable, more positively motivated, when constant competition and the anxiety it entails are eliminated, or at least reduced, and classmates become a source of mutual help. In this atmosphere, students can anticipate ultimate success in their efforts and not be afraid of failing or falling below someone else's level of achievement. There is constant communication, facilitated by free movement in the classroom, and this creates a relaxed and gratifying social environment. Students are released from the tension of being constantly watched and judged and of having to keep rules of behavior.

An active planning-and-learning role for the student necessitates a complementary change in the role of the teacher. From being a dispenser and transmitter of knowledge, he becomes a guide and advisor to students. He helps them investigate issues and clarify and solve problems; but he is not the main source of information, nor the absolute judge of what is correct and incorrect. He continues to play an important role in planning and selecting the materials which make up a large part of the learning environment, including the way in which the students can organize themselves for learning purposes. Students need guidance in order to have instructive experiences; but it is actually the adoption of a nondirective role by the teacher which is prerequisite for changing the pupil's posture from a passive-receptive one to an active decision-making and responsibility-sharing one. To achieve this the teacher (according to the Dewey-Piaget model) must recognize the possibility, perhaps even the necessity, of stimulating students to learn by letting them work out solutions or investigate problems in their own way, at their own pace, and without constant control.

Finally, a note about the role of the curriculum. In an educational setting which fosters an active learning role for the student, the chief purpose of the curriculum is to help the teacher select general topic areas at appropriate developmental levels for the class. The curriculum should not become a contract with requirements to be rigidly fulfilled. It must not *limit*, but *stimulate*, the teacher in the search for projects and activities which will engage the students. It must be a set of flexible guidelines with a wide latitude of freedom for students to plan their own activities. The knowledge of what students have studied in the past and are likely to study in the future will help teachers approach new concepts at an appropriate level. That can be the curriculum's greatest contribution (Wickens, 1973).

What Is a Group?

In the following pages of this chapter we offer some explanations as to why the organization of students into small groups for learning purposes is so admirably suited for implementing the educational values presented above. But before discussing what small groups can accomplish, we must answer a fundamental question, namely: What is a group? Does a group differ from the usual class of pupils? After all, isn't the class *also* a group? Does the number of students alone distinguish a class from a group?

A number of people gathered together in a particular place do not *ipso facto* constitute a group. As long as they do not have any mutual exchange, or work together for some larger purpose, they remain a collection of unrelated individuals. A group is comprised of interdependent individuals with mutual relatedness in their activities and a common goal (Gibb, 1969). The groups discussed in this book are those devoted to achieving learning goals, such as investigating issues or solving problems.

We can now understand the radical difference between small-group teaching and ability grouping, with which it is sometimes unjustly compared. Ability grouping seeks to ease the teacher's task by creating a relatively homogeneous student body, in terms of level of intelligence or achievement in a particular subject; but it does not imply any essential change in the pattern of relationships among students or between teachers and students during their learning efforts. It does not impose any alteration in the expository manner in which teachers present learning materials, or in the passive-receptive manner in which students are expected to learn them, which characterize traditional teaching and learning.

Small-group teaching, on the other hand, is an approach to classroom organization, encompassing a wide variety of techniques, for structuring the relationships of students and teachers. It changes the very way in which pupils and teachers behave when engaged in learning and teaching and the kinds of roles they fill. Small-group teaching is not aimed at selecting WHO participates in a particular learning session, but at structuring HOW the participants will learn.

In small-group teaching, the larger class of pupils breaks up into smaller groups. This division is usually very flexible. Groups continue to function only as long as they are working toward a specific goal. Even during the period of its existence, the membership of a group may change if students find it desirable. Groups are rarely if ever homogeneous in terms of IQ or academic achievement, though students with similar learning needs can be grouped together at times to improve specific skills, if and when that becomes necessary. Rather, groups are usually formed on the basis of the students' interest in studying a particular problem or topic, or on the basis of friendships. (The subject of group composition is discussed in Chapter Two of this book.) Here we wish to emphasize that the aim of small groups is to foster cooperation and communication among students for learning purposes, and to create a social context for individual investigation and involvement.

Advantages of Small Groups

The major advantages of small groups are in the following areas: the social and emotional effects of small-group teaching; the effect of the small group on the kind of learning; the development of logical thought and verbal communication; and the reevaluation of the role of teacher and student.

One fundamental goal of small-group teaching is to help students find expression for their abilities. Individuality is the most important contribution a student can make to a group. When he feels that he can communicate directly with his classmates, when he knows that he not only may, but is even expected to cooperate with others, then the group is already exerting a strong positive influence on his learning experience. His motivation to work together with other group members is increased, and he develops positive attitudes toward group activities (Collins and Guetzkow, 1964; Gibb, 1969; Kelley and Thibaut, 1969; Thelen, 1954). Students who participate in cooperative groups tend to view their studies as *work*, rather than as *labor*; they see their teacher as a counselor and advisor, rather than as a task-master or policeman—words often used by students in traditional classrooms (Thelen, 1954).

Freedom to communicate with others in word and action creates a relaxed atmosphere and a contrast to the one-group classroom, in which the criteria for acceptable behavior are silence and rigid attention. Students in small groups are free to walk around and to converse with others, as in most social settings. Mental ease, calm, and absence of tension enable students to approach work creatively, while pressure and critical analysis have the opposite effect. Many observers have commented that this atmosphere injects students with a joy of learning which is sorely missing in the formal school environment (Blackie, 1971; Blitz, 1973; Gardner, 1966; Silberman, 1970; Thelen, 1954). The pleasant atmosphere in groups also stems from a feeling of cooperation among students, as opposed to the tension-producing competitive character of formal classes. Students in cooperative groups expect to succeed in their work, and this expectation eliminates much of the anxiety which plagues so many students throughout their school career.

Small-group teaching draws some of its motivating power from the creation of a social context for learning. The very differences between personalities, which formal teaching tends to ignore, bring interest and a wide range of knowledge and skills to the group. In formal classrooms, uniform standards and requirements often are set up for everyone. Small-group learning, on the other hand, cultivates respect for each person's unique contribution to the collective effort. Students learn that they can say what they think about a topic and do not need to conform to one dominant opinion. The different interests, backgrounds, values, and abilities of the members are, in fact, the group's greatest asset and the source of its potentially creative learning experiences.

Students who participated in one small-group teaching experiment said that the experience helped them to establish friendships with their classmates more easily, to be more confident socially, and to express themselves in public without inhibition. These students participated in groups in which the leadership was rotated regularly and everyone had a chance to perform some administrative function. Many pupils were gratified to find that they could chair meetings successfully, and although there were occasional disciplinary problems that they could not handle, the positive nature of the group experience was clearly demonstrated (Meehan and Schusler, 1966).

Cooperation in planning group activities is another advantage of this method. At the start, the group must work out a fairly detailed plan of procedure, which must cover more than just the subject under study, whether it be for research, discussion, dramatic presentation, or a game. The general subject should be subdivided into clearly defined topics and subtopics, with specific tasks and roles assigned to each member. This procedure involves students directly in decisions regarding the content of their study, and thereby increases the degree of responsibility they are prepared to assume for their own learning. They are more likely to have a mature attitude when they are partners in the decision-making process than when most of the important decisions have already been made by some authority. Involvement in the planning of their education will help them develop their intellectual interests, and this in turn will give them a chance to strive for adult goals and not be locked into a peer culture with less mature, more child-oriented values. Making students intellectually dependent on adults for all decisions in school can retard their intellectual development and may even cause them to regard learning as childish (Glidewell, 1966).

In our view, one of the most critical challenges to classroom teaching is how to help students become involved in their learning experiences and to assume a large measure of personal responsibility for these experiences. A feeling of genuine involvement does not develop when students have no control over their school activities, and no share in decision-making. Being pawns in the hands of authority, being told constantly what and how to learn, what and when to perform, breeds apathy and alienation, sometimes even active resistance. Effective participation in influencing classroom life leads to favorable attitudes toward school, increased willingness to learn, and greater investment of effort in carrying out school tasks (De Charms, 1968, 1971; Solomon and Oberlander, 1974; White and Howard, 1970).

Small groups are an effective organizational medium for encouraging, clarifying, and guiding student participation in planning classroom activities, both academic and social. They provide a means of practicing democratic leadership so that students do not feel constantly under the control of a higher authority. Instead, they can share in influencing the nature of events which take place in school—where they spend such a significant portion of their lives. The techniques described in this book emphasize the role of the teacher as guide and resource person for students in their cooperative efforts at planning and carrying out productive and rewarding experiences in school.

We believe that one salient reason why so many students in so many countries at best tolerate, or worse, dislike school is that schools control and manipulate them, in contrast with their lives outside school, in which they enjoy a large measure of self-direction. Inside school, events are made to happen by others; while outside, the student often is the active agent and he himself makes events happen. By restoring to students their more human role as causal agents, schools can restore to their students dignity and the joy of acting and learning (Harré and Secord, 1973).

Small-Group Learning
and Academic Achievement

If group members communicate freely and can cooperate effectively in their chosen tasks, they can achieve more than they would as individuals. The final result of their work, be it a written or verbal report, a display, an experiment, or an artistic creation, can be more informed, more accurate, and intellectually richer than work done individually by the same people (Collins and Guetzkow, 1964; Davis, 1969; Kelley and Thibaut, 1969; Lott and Lott, 1966).

It would be wrong to suggest that group work be substituted for all individual work. Both group and individual learning are important for the development of human resources. The point here is that the personal contact made possible by the small group, and the range of different abilities, motivate group members to work together and enable them to solve problems they could not have solved alone. Groups have distinct advantages over individuals in solving problems which can be broken down into smaller units. They can deal with them from more points of view and in less time than individuals. Also, when one student finishes his part, he can help another.

An important conclusion is that it is not always possible to know from any one student's performance as an individual how he will behave as a group member. True, there is no such thing as a "group mind," nor does the group itself "learn" apart from what each member learns. However, the network of relations within the group does create a social, emotional, and intellectual *context* for learning—a context which exerts considerable influence on the way individuals learn, on how and what they learn, and on their attitudes toward learning. This learning environment differs radically from one in which students are unable to cooperate.

There are many groups whose results are not superior to those of work done by individuals in the group (Hudgins, 1960; Hudgins and Smith, 1966), but even so, traditional teaching does not surpass teaching with small groups. When students in traditional classrooms and in small cooperative groups are given standard achievement tests, the traditional method does not prove to be superior to the small-group approach. It should be remembered, however, that standard achievement tests do not assess the kind of learning progress fostered by the small-group approach. Most older research findings indicate that, even by traditional educational standards (primarily in terms of quantities of knowledge) small-group learning is not inferior. Small groups exert a positive influence on students' attitudes toward study, which is not cultivated in traditional classrooms (Boocock and Coleman, 1966; Davis, 1969; Gardner, 1966; Haigh and Schmidt, 1956; Heinkel, 1970; Kelley and Thibaut, 1969). Moreover, results from recent observations of eighteen thousand classrooms in the United States indicate that small-group teaching has distinct advantages over traditional teaching for achieving educational excellence (Olson, 1971; see also Dunkin and Biddle, 1974).

It is possible too that small groups encourage a more abstract level of thought than does traditional, receptive learning. The group analyzes and evaluates each member's contribution to the solution of the problem, and various contributions are synthesized into a final group product. Individual members gather information and ideas to present to the group, but all members cooperate in analyzing the information and weaving it into a meaningful statement. These features of group learning involve students in activities which are more complex, more intellectually stimulating, and more sophisticated than the receptive learning typical of traditional schools. The analysis, synthesis, and evaluation of information and ideas are generally acknowledged to constitute higher levels of intellectual functioning than those required of students when asked to acquire and understand given quantities of knowledge (Bloom *et al.*, 1956).

The evidence that small groups can contribute substantially to intellectual development is scanty but provocative. It comes from two areas: the development of verbal expression and the development of logical thinking.

Schools everywhere place great importance on pupils' ability to express their thoughts, and the development of expressive skills is a major educational goal. Why, then, do students still sit in rows and listen to the teacher talk, while for most of the day they are supposed to remain silent? Verbal expression is, in its very essence, a social activity; yet in formal education social contacts in the classroom are usually not sanctioned. The nature of people's social relationships also influences the nature of their conversation and even determines whether conversation will take place at all. A pupil's very willingness to express himself, as well as his level of communication, depends on the social role he is expected to fulfill in school: a passive-receptive or an active, decision-making role; that of one expected to talk or of one expected to listen.

The quality of verbal expression of culturally disadvantaged children has been shown to change markedly according to the role they occupy at any given time (as could be expected of anyone!). In a role-playing session with culturally disadvantaged children, one group played the role of teachers, who were seen as talkers, and another played the role of pupils, who were seen as listeners. Change of role from listener to talker was accompanied by a distinct change in the level of language spoken by the children. In the role of teacher, they used richer language and longer, more complex sentences (Herbert, 1970; Reissman, 1962).

Social roles in the classroom influence the children's speech in other ways, too. Pupils know that their remarks are evaluated by teachers, so they employ the strategy of giving short, non-committal answers to questions, thus avoiding giving inaccurate information or saying something which might displease the teacher. When the pupil's role is changed, these inhibitions can disappear. Taking the pupil out of his passive role of listener and consumer of information, and putting *him* in the active role of a team member can draw out expressive abilities.

Piaget asserts that interaction between children is one of the chief motivations of their intellectual development. It is important that they be exposed to points of view different from their own so that, gradually, they will examine their environment more objectively and not only from their perspective. Even very young children evince great curiosity about their social environment. They want to understand the behavior of people in various roles and are keen to assimilate information about them and to imitate such roles as parents, teachers, doctors, firemen, and painters. The child's social life is clearly an important force in his intellectual as well as emotional development (Piaget, 1951, 1970; Piaget and Inhelder, 1969).

It is still not known how children advance from their typically subjective way of thinking to a more mature and objective mode of thought. One intriguing suggestion is that a child's conviction that his own perspective is the correct one is disturbed by a conflict with the view of someone else (usually someone of about his own age), which occurs when his own view fails to account for obvious facts, and when he is able to see reason in the other view. This situation stimulates the child to consider the other view, thereby reaching a broader, less subjective level of understanding (Langer, 1969; Piaget, 1926; Piaget and Inhelder, 1969; Smedslund, 1966). Since the "conflict" arises from information obtained by contact with other children, attempts have been made to find out if such an intellectually stimulating situation can be created through group interaction.

In the following experiment (Murray, 1972), groups of three children of kindergarten age were formed. Three beakers were placed before a child. Beakers #1 and #2 were of equal size and contained the same amount of water. Beaker #3 was empty and differed in height and width from the other two. After confirmation that the two identical beakers contained equal quantities of water, the water from beaker #1 was poured into beaker #3 and the child was asked if beakers #3 and #2 now contained the same or different amounts of liquid. In each group one child was able to solve the problem, while the other two were not (they believed that beaker #3 contained a different amount of water from beaker #2). The children were told they would not get a score for their solution unless a correct answer was reached unanimously.

Everyone was free to use all the equipment as much as necessary and to experiment by pouring water from one beaker to the other; but the teacher was not to give hints or information of any sort. A week after the experiment took place all of the 57 participants were tested individually to see what they had learned, but the test used different materials from those used in the experiment.

The outcome was quite remarkable. Many children who were not able to solve the problem at first, were able to do so after their experience in the group. Not only did the group discussion (which created a "conflict" between differing views of the problem) improve the reasoning of the children who favored the idea of non-conservation, it also improved the *quality* of the solution and the explanation given by the children who could solve the problem from the start. Thus, everyone in the group gained something from interaction with other pupils, each according to his own level of understanding. It is important to note that there was no "teaching" in this experiment—all learning was a result of group discussion and experimentation. The comment of a student in another group-learning experiment helps to clarify the process: "We examine the answers together, compare them, and see what happens" (Meehan and Schusler, 1966; see also Laughlin, 1965; Laughlin and Doherty, 1967; Laughlin, McGlynn, *et al.*, 1968).

Teacher and Student Roles

In a small-group classroom the *learning process* becomes the main focus of the teacher's attention. Preparation of materials still occupies his or her thought and time, but is closely related to the way in which a given activity is planned. A teaching plan is no longer synonymous with deciding what ideas to teach *about* a subject. It must be accompanied by plans of *how the students* will use the material in their learning activities.

Students' roles also change in this new learning environment. They must be helped to acquire the social skills they need for cooperative learning, as opposed to the competitive race for grades. They must learn to do independent research as part of a larger group project, to formulate their findings, to help place their work in the context of the work of others, and to conduct themselves in this setting without being under the vigilant eye of authority. Students are removed from their roles as "learning machines" with constant input and output and become instead active planners and deciders. These changes can make school a more pleasant place for teachers and students alike and increase the efficiency of the school as a whole.

The Promise and Problems
of Small-Group Teaching

Small-group teaching holds much promise if used thoughtfully. It promises to serve as a major alternative to the expository teaching and verbal-receptive learning which continue to bore many pupils and teachers in schools today (Barth, 1972; Sarason, 1971; Silberman, 1970). It promises to provide a planned, moderately structured set of techniques for implementing democratic education without deteriorating into an aimless permissiveness. It is based upon, and carefully plans for, the active involvement of students in planning and carrying out intellectually stimulating tasks. These are its main goals as well as its criteria for effectiveness. Whether these techniques can in fact achieve the goals intended for them is a question for future research. In one of the most thorough reviews to date of research on teaching, the authors conclude: ". . . the ideal teaching situation is neither that of pupils in isolation or the class as a whole but rather that of small, supervised groups" (Dunkin and Biddle, 1974, p. 213).

What problems should teachers anticipate in small-group teaching? Every classroom is a complex social system with a host of problems for the educator, and every teaching method or combination of methods constitutes a challenge to the teacher's ingenuity for problem-solving. A small-group approach to teaching offers a fruitful alternative to traditional classroom organization, but it also presents the teacher with its own set of problems. These fall into three main categories: interaction, organization, and coordination. Although they overlap, these concepts can provide helpful guidelines for anticipating potential sources of difficulty. Close attention to them can produce striking improvements in a group's ability to work together and achieve the goals of its members.

Problems of interaction. The quality of the relationships among members will determine how the group will function. The nature of communication, the extent to which members like each other and want to belong to the group, the amount of satisfaction they gain from contributing to its progress, are all factors which influence the group's experience.

It is a fact of everyday life that people do not always listen attentively to what others are saying to them. Often we do not even listen to what we are saying to others! Cooperative group work requires members to engage in a productive give-and-take, which implies attentive listening to what others are saying. Furthermore, listening means controlling one's own speech and letting other members express their ideas and feelings. One of the more obvious problems of group interaction is that discussion can be dominated by a few members, with others withdrawing to let the more outspoken students take over. The issue of domineering versus more reserved students is, of course, endemic to every form of classroom organization, but since one of the major goals of small-group teaching is to involve most—if not all—of the students in the learning process, it is imperative that a resolution be found in the small-group classroom.

In any large group (such as a classroom) some people will enjoy higher status than others. High status is accorded for a wide number of reasons, many connected with the wider social values, such as getting high grades in school, having a high IQ, being a star in sports, or belonging to a high-status rather than a minority ethnic group. High-status persons tend to dominate group activities at the expense of others, whose opinions or wishes may be either ignored or not even expressed in the presence of higher-status students. It is utopian to strive for completely equal-status interaction among group members, but teachers can help groups to develop increasingly equitable behavior as the group progresses (Cohen, 1973; Cohen and Roper, 1972).

Problems of organization. Whenever several people work together, organizational problems will arise. In the traditional classroom they usually pertain to the way the teacher functions, how he or she presents material, how he or she organizes students. In the small-group classroom, organizational issues must be dealt with by the groups themselves in order to facilitate their own progress.

The primary problems of organization are often the selection and clarification of the group task, specifying procedures for gathering relevant information, and achieving fair distribution of work among group members or different groups. Even if the general topic is determined by the teacher (or by the curriculum), the groups themselves must decide on the specific aspects to be investigated. Next, potential resources must be located and access to them arranged. Finally, subtopics must be divided among group members in such a way that they feel both interested in their specific project and aware of its relevance to the wider group goal.

Usually there is more than one group in the classroom, and teachers must deal with the organizational problems of all of them. This may involve obtaining access to needed resources, be they books, laboratory demonstrations or facilities, experts outside the school, libraries in or outside the school, tools, or materials; it may also involve setting up time schedules for each group, as well as for the class as a whole. In the upper grades of elementary school, both of these procedures should be part of the groups' responsibilities, but younger students will have to rely more upon the teacher's direction.

Problems of coordination. Problems of coordination arise within each group as well as between different groups. Coordination between groups is important if more than one group investigates one problem or different aspects of it. Who will investigate what (both within one group or among different groups)? How will the various efforts be integrated or presented? These are the major issues of coordination. Will only one report be prepared on the group work? Will some members work together on research and presentation of their findings, while others work individually and contribute their results to the final group report? Will some prepare an exhibition and others a written report, a dramatization, or a laboratory demonstration? Coordination of individual efforts should be planned so that the group can present a summary of its work in some fashion. The way in which coordination is accomplished can contribute a great deal to the students' gratification at having been group members, and strengthen their motivation to work in groups in the future.

The following chapters are aimed at helping teachers to face and solve these problems, and the book focuses mainly on the problems of organization and coordination, although there are also many suggestions for dealing with problems of interaction. For additional help on interaction, the excellent books by Gorman (1969), Johnson (1972), Johnson and Johnson (1975), and Napier and Gershenfeld (1973) can be consulted. Most of all, we hope that the ideas and methods presented here will stimulate teachers to complement this material with the products of their own inventiveness.

Chapter Two

How Small Groups Work

A fundamental aspect of most classrooms is that they are inhabited five (or six) days a week, for several hours at a time, by a group usually numbering from 25 to 45 persons. Sometimes many of these people proceed together from one grade to the next through the years of their compulsory education. Students clearly have more opportunity to know each other well and interact in a wide variety of situations than do people in almost any other social institution. It is natural for people who meet so frequently and for such long hours to evolve complex networks of social relations. Indeed, the average classroom contains many subgroups formed on the basis of friendship patterns, mutual interests, social class membership, residential areas, etc. (Bany and Johnson, 1964; Glidewell, 1966). Ironically, traditional education views social contact between students within the classroom setting as a peripheral phenomenon of school life, even as potentially disruptive of learning. Rarely is this social contact utilized as one of the most powerful tools for fostering learning. By contrast, cooperation and communication between students is the primary vehicle of the educational process in the model of teaching and learning being presented here. The dynamics of small-group behavior, the way in which people in small groups relate to each other and learn to cooperate, are not merely a by-product of the classroom situation. Rather, they are a key to achieving the more important goals of teaching and learning.

This chapter discusses several issues in group dynamics which are relevant to small-group teaching. For the sake of clarity, these issues have been divided into five categories: (1) social relations, (2) communication, (3) selection of members and tasks, (4) group leadership, and (5) group development. In life, however, these factors affect group activities simultaneously, each factor influencing the other. For example, communication between group members is determined by how they get along with each other, by how the chairman leads the group discussion, and by the nature of the topic which the group is investigating. Being aware of these issues will help teachers use small groups more effectively, to understand potential sources of difficulty in group functioning, and to find ways to facilitate group processes so the group can achieve its goals and be a source of gratification to its members.

Social Relations

The effect of group friendship patterns. Friendly or hostile relationships within the group exert far-reaching effects on the academic performance of its members. Social and emotional factors influence more than the children's emotional adjustment in school. Students who are accepted by their classmates generally realize their potential and achieve academic success more readily than students who feel rejected or neglected by classmates (Glidewell, 1966; Hartup, 1970; Lippitt and Gold, 1959; Schmuck, 1966).

Students are constantly evaluating each other, even if their reactions are not verbalized. Why we like or dislike certain people is influenced by many factors. The reasons for our emotional relationships are determined not only by how well we know someone, but also by factors of background, such as class, ethnic origin, and level and type of education. All social relations are strongly influenced by *expectations* regarding people's behavior—apparently molded in the course of time—and not simply by *actual* behavior. The fact that people take an immediate liking to some and react negatively to others when they join a small group shows that friendships are frequently formed on the basis of preconceived ideas, and not merely on a wait-and-see basis. This is as true of children in school as it is of adults in the larger society (Hartup, 1970; Pope, 1953). Understanding children's social relations is therefore critical to understanding their school behavior in general and their academic performance in particular.

Classrooms can be divided into two typical categories with regard to friendship patterns. In the first, friendships are concentrated on a few "stars," while most of the other pupils are left out (though not necessarily rejected). In the second, friendships are widely distributed and there are almost no outstanding "stars." Those classrooms where friendships are concentrated in a few students are largely of the traditional type, where teaching is mainly in the form of lectures, there are many examinations, and only a few students are called upon to rècite. The teacher—often covertly—supports the status of the "star" pupils, perhaps in order to seek popularity for himself or herself by expressing approval of the popular students. Because of their formal teaching method, it is precisely this popularity which traditional teachers often lack. In this environment, the concentrated friendship pattern thrives (Johnson, 1970; Schmuck, 1963; Schmuck and Schmuck, 1971).

All people are concerned with their social status, and students, eager to be accepted by classmates, are no exception. But when eagerness becomes anxiety over whether they are accepted by their peers, their learning ability may be disrupted. Students test their social standing among classmates in different ways, and are curious to learn how others see them. When classroom friendships are expressed toward a select few, it is relatively easy to estimate whether one belongs to the accepted or the not-so-accepted group. Those left outside the circle of "desirable" friends are vulnerable to negative feelings about themselves: they feel they may be less able, less worthy, or less talented than those closer to the centers of friendship (or centers of power). Students on the social periphery are likely to regard the classroom as threatening. On the other hand, when friendships are widely diffused, fewer students feel neglected, and the popularity scale is no longer a convenient measure of social status (Schmuck, 1963, 1966; Schmuck and Schmuck, 1971).

Small-group teaching can promote diffuse friendships in the classroom, as friendships are more likely to be shared by all or most members of a small group, where there is more opportunity for constructive cooperation among members, than in a large group. Small groups can stimulate mutuality, instead of the competitive atmosphere common to traditional classrooms.

Group cohesiveness. A cohesive group is one whose members want to work together. There are two main groups of factors influencing group cohesiveness:

1. Members hold particular personal attraction for each other (for reasons of ability, interests, appearance, or status), so that they enjoy working with one another, support each other on a personal basis, and desire to maintain contact with other members.
2. The tasks of the group coincide with the individuals' own goals, values, or interests. Furthermore, the members recognize that they are more likely to achieve their own goals by cooperating with others than by working individually (Cartwright and Zander, 1968).

Every group must have a minimum of cohesiveness in order to function as a unit. Without it, the group will disintegrate, which means that its members will try to work alone, with no cooperation. Groups with high cohesiveness succeed in agreeing upon common goals and in working together to implement them. Participants listen to each other's opinions and are prepared to alter their behavior in light of others' suggestions more than in groups with low cohesiveness (Berkowitz, 1954; Shaw, 1971). Group cohesiveness influences interaction among members, productivity, and the degree of satisfaction experienced from belonging to the group (Collins and Raven, 1969; Shaw, 1971). Let us examine these features in greater detail.

We interact with people to whom, for some reason, we are attracted. Obviously the *amount* of interaction between two people depends, in part, on the frequency of their meetings: we cannot interact much with someone we seldom see. Surprisingly, however, this factor alone does not determine the extent of interaction. Interaction among group members is dependent upon how much they like each other and not only on how often they meet (Lott and Lott, 1961).

In the following study with groups of second-grade children, three-member groups, each with a different degree of cohesiveness, were asked to engage in a *cooperative* spelling task. The teachers observing the groups were not told about the extent of cohesiveness in each. The children in groups with a high degree of cohesiveness displayed greater friendship and cooperation toward each other. They praised other group members for their efforts, and cooperative planning for solving the group task was evident, as was a high level of participation by all members. Furthermore, the chairmen of these groups behaved democratically, respecting the integrity of each individual. Group members also spent time together socially.

The groups with low-cohesiveness depicted quite a different picture. Members quarreled and were hostile to each other. Some expressed glee at others' mistakes, and were more concerned with testing others' spelling than with planning together to cope with the task. The chairmen acted in an authoritarian manner, giving orders to members. Finally, the groups began to splinter, and separate individuals tried to study by themselves, with no interest in what others were doing (Shaw and Shaw, 1962).

Group cohesiveness is not necessarily a precondition for cooperation among pupils. Experiences in cooperation can themselves increase group cohesiveness. When groups engage in cooperative tasks requiring interdependence of members, they are more likely to form friendly ties and influence each other than when the task stimulates competition among members (Deutsch, 1968). Actual accomplishment of the task also increases group cohesiveness. Membership in a social body which cannot realize its own goals is not valued (Davis, 1969).

Cohesiveness, therefore, is a much needed quality of groups. It can be systematically planned and developed as part of the group's activities, and its presence enhances the group's ability to work toward its learning goals. (Specific steps to improve cohesiveness will be discussed throughout ensuing chapters: see particularly Chapter Four.) In any case, absence of cohesiveness at the outset of a group's formation is not cause for discouragement nor for disbanding the group; it will probably function satisfactorily with proper guidance and training. Procedures and skills for cooperative learning are acquired with experience; they are not natural endowments, any more than is the task of sitting at a desk for long stretches of time. Students who are accustomed to a traditional classroom setting may even have difficulty making the transition to cooperative group learning, but the positive effects of group cohesiveness certainly justify the time spent on planning the proper experiences. The benefits are increased friendliness among group members and greater gratification of the students' need for acceptance by classmates. It is this acceptance which sets the stage for genuine cooperation among students; and cooperation is necessary in order to achieve productive learning. Cohesiveness is also enhanced when group members derive both educational and social satisfaction from belonging to a group. They are gratified to know that their participation contributes to the group's progress.

Group norms. Group members hold different values about learning, and these serve as group norms, or shared sets of expectations and attitudes which influence learning behavior. People generally conform to norms accepted by their peers. If norms in relation to learning procedures were discussed openly, most participants would cooperate. It is advisable, therefore, for groups to devote some time to discussing questions concerning research procedures and learning methods.

Usually, students learn about research *results*, about the conclusions others have reached through their intellectual efforts. Rarely do schools present the research process itself as a form of study, and students are not conscious of the *process* of acquiring knowledge. Learning can be enhanced enormously if small groups clarify the basic principles of research appropriate to their current task. In other words, rather than merely gathering information *about* a given subject, students should actually do research *into* it, thereby making it more realistic. They should practice the discipline itself as far as possible. This manner of study promotes positive learning norms and emphasizes personal involvement and responsibility. It also embodies the practical meaning of Dewey's educational philosophy.

Group norms affect students' social as well as academic behavior. Rules for conduct should also be discussed by the group and accepted by participants. Early clarification of expectations about conduct by the group itself can minimize interpersonal conflict, maximize goal-directed behavior, and render any disciplinary intervention by the teacher unnecessary. Group norms can be an effective source of social control to enable efficient use of the group's research time. Norms are more effectively presented in open discussion than when simply handed out by figures in authority (Levine and Butler, 1952; McKeachie, 1954; Schmuck and Schmuck, 1971; Sherif, 1936).

Here are six basic ways to promote positive group norms for classroom learning (Johnson, 1970):

1. Students are likely to accept those norms which they relate clearly to their own goals. Teachers should clarify these relationships fairly often.
2. Students will identify with norms they helped to draft themselves. Norms should be determined democratically with the participation of all students.

3. The number of norms must be kept to a minimum and must be absolutely necessary for the group's ability to function. An excess of rules and regulations stifles student creativity and generates an unpleasant classroom atmosphere.
4. An atmosphere of cooperation and mutual trust in the classroom promotes the students' acceptance of norms.
5. The norms must be flexible and should be changed when necessary. They are for the benefit of the students, not the teacher.
6. Desirable norms are developed by providing examples and supporting behavior patterns which reflect them.

Communication

Communication in the traditional classroom is usually uni-directional—from teacher to pupil. Sometimes it becomes recipro-cal, so that the student also addresses the teacher; but even this two-directional communication is primarily in the form of questions by the teacher and answers by the student, and only rarely does it evolve into a genuine conversation. During most of the school hours, students are not supposed to converse among themselves; any inter-pupil communication is usually mediated by the teacher, and this places the teacher under constant demand from students for recognition and permission to speak. Indeed, many teachers complain that students demand too much atten-tion, and ironically, it is the organization of the traditional classroom which creates this pressure, not the personalities of the pupils.

Teaching in small groups can stimulate genuine conversation among students. Such classrooms are certainly noisier than the traditional classroom. Six or seven small groups in one classroom, actively engaged in cooperative learning tasks, will generate a reasonable level of noise, and teachers who are accustomed to relative quiet will have to adjust to the noise of activity and recognize its positive features. It is easy to distinguish between productive and disruptive noise. The students themselves can make rules for evaluating and controlling the noise level, as well as for regulating conduct. It is generally acknowledged that when students take an active part in the learning process, problems of behavior control are markedly reduced in contrast with the traditional setting.

In a study of the effects of different interaction patterns on two types of groups (Bovard, 1956), one group engaged in open discussion, and everyone sat in a circle, including the teacher, who behaved like a member of the group. A second group conducted a more formal discussion, with the teacher standing in front of the group and giving students permission to speak in turn. Students in the open discussion group expressed their opinions more freely and addressed each other when speaking. They made many more spontaneous contributions to the group task and were generally more active than those in the formal group. Moreover, pupils in the open discussion formed friendships with one another more easily and influenced each other more readily than those in the formal group. Students in the traditional class did not communicate with each other, nor did they evince much spontaneity, and group cohesiveness was decidedly lower than in the open discussion group. Thus, friendship patterns, the free exchange of ideas and feelings among students, multi-directional communication, and group cohesiveness combine to have a powerful effect on group functioning.

Free discussion in the group does not mean that there is no longer any direction from the teacher. The students will need guidance in planning and evaluating their activities. It is *constant* control by the teacher which prevents the groups from learning the social skills needed for productive group functioning. Preferably, pupils themselves should assume responsibility for directing their activities, but the teacher should ensure that students treat each other equitably and supportively. He or she can also promote efficient group work by helping pupils to clarify goals and to focus evaluation on the group's products and not on the contributions of individual members. If particular students dominate the group, the teacher can find ways to activate those who are less talkative and contain the domineering ones. Role playing (Chapter Seven), for example, can help retiring students become more active and give more vocal students insight into their own behavior. An over-active student could be asked to observe and report the group's progress without talking during the discussion. The nature of communication in the group should be discussed so that the group reaches greater understanding of its own functioning; such discussions can also enhance group cohesiveness.

Communication among pupils is also facilitated by group members' being able to sit close enough to one another to maximize eye contact. Eye-contact influences the flow and quality of verbal communication (Argyle, 1967; Argyle and Dean, 1965; Sommer, 1967). The frequent eye contact permitted by the small-group setting helps to foster closer ties among its members than is possible in large groups.

Group size. Communication in the group is influenced in both quality and quantity by its size (Hare, 1952, 1962). Small groups promote self-expression and allow each student to learn in the way most appropriate to him. Students do not feel compelled to proceed at the set pace of a large group (as is frequently the case in classrooms numbering anywhere from 25 to 45 students). The group must, on the other hand, be large enough for productive exchange of ideas among students with different viewpoints or skills. Size should be planned according to goals.

Group size also influences the extent of members' involvement in the group's progress. When only a handful of pupils work together, each feels more responsible and the motivational power of group membership is intensified. However, a small number of group members limits the range of human resources (general fund of knowledge, special skills, experiential background, etc.) which could enrich the group's cooperative efforts and diversify the viewpoints. These different effects of group size must be considered carefully (Davis, 1969; Shaw, 1971; Steiner, 1972).

The optimal number of participants in a small learning group is a matter for discussion. Some claim that it is between five and eight persons, others as many as 15. Simple calculation proves that the number of possible interactions increases geometrically as the number of group members increases arithmetically.

Three people can generate six channels of communication; in a four-member group, the number of possible communications jumps to 12. The remarkable fact, however, is that as the number of members increases beyond the small-group stage, the frequency of times each one speaks declines, and so does the *total amount* of conversation in the group (Dawe, 1934). Obviously, large groups do not foster interpersonal communication and not only because each person has less time to express himself. Members of large groups do not participate as spontaneously as those in smaller groups.

In groups of eight members, each one addresses himself to the group as a unit. But when there are more than eight in the group, individuals contribute less than would be expected. The gap in the amount of communication between the dominant members and those who are more passive also widens. The larger the group the greater the danger that it will revert to a traditional classroom, in which a few pupils monopolize the recitations (Gibb, 1951; Hare, 1962; Institute for Development of Educational Activities, 1971; Thelen, 1949; Thelen, 1954).

The optimum number of group members, therefore, seems to be between five and eight pupils. If a long discussion is involved, probably the number should not exceed six; but, of course, this suggestion cannot be a hard and fast rule. When deciding the appropriate group size, consideration must always be given to the nature of the task. Flexible use of larger and smaller groups may be productive during role playing (see Chapter Seven) or simulation games (see Chapter Eight), when many roles must be represented, and small groups of students could present different factions, parties, or interests.

Spatial placement of group members. Seating arrangement influences communication in the group. Small-group teaching requires completely different seating plans from those of the traditional classroom. The aim is to maximize face-to-face contact, rather than the face-to-back arrangement. Since the teacher of small groups is not merely a dispenser of knowledge, but rather a guide and counselor, rearrangement of the seating plan and the redefinition of the teacher's role are complementary. On the other hand, alteration of the seating arrangement alone cannot guarantee increased communication among pupils. A teacher can continue to monopolize the conversation even when pupils sit in a circle, and there may be no real change in communication. In order to transform the class from a collection of individuals into many cooperative groups, the teacher must cut down his or her own rate of talking and *stimulate students* to improve their communication.

Selection of Members and Tasks

The task. How do students and teachers plan group projects so each member feels he has shared in their adoption and implementation? The solution entails careful examination of a topic in order to subdivide it into individual research items. Everyone in the group must be able to make his own contribution to the final group product. Each student (or pairs of students, depending on how they decide to proceed) must feel that it is inherently rewarding and informative for him to investigate that particular subtopic. Clearly, subjects which lend themselves to this kind of treatment must be relatively complex and usually open to a variety of interpretations. A detailed example of a project suggested and subdivided by the class into meaningful subparts for group investigation appears in Chapter Four.

Unitary tasks which cannot be subdivided are not appropriate for group work. Examples of unitary tasks would be a question to which there is a direct right or wrong answer, a question requiring a single piece of information as a reply, or any problem which can be solved only by going through all the steps in order to arrive at a solution, such as is required by many mathematical problems. Such tasks might be more profitably solved under conditions of completely individualized instruction rather than as a group project. This does not mean, of course, that mathematical problems cannot be a part of a group project. For example, different group members might solve different problems, and then compare the methods each one used. It does mean that single, indivisible problems generally are not appropriate for group study (Steiner, 1972).

Productive group work depends, of course, on more than just dividing up a subject among members. A group needs experience in working together to learn how to utilize its human resources. It needs experience in cooperative planning, experience in making mistakes in organization and operation, and experience in analyzing mistakes so as to improve group efficiency. It needs the experience of discussing its own procedures in order to promote the members' awareness of their group role. This exercise can often be helpful to a group whose work is not progressing, reorienting members to their common purpose. Teachers should anticipate that groups will not always function at their best, and be prepared to reorganize when necessary. Failure to achieve all the ideals of group learning is no cause for assuming that traditional teaching methods are more reliable. Nor is the solving of organizational and procedural problems irrelevant to learning. The students should be made to feel confident of achieving important objectives with the necessary patience, direction, and guidance from the teacher.

In the early stages of its formation a group will depend heavily on the teacher's help. With this help, independent functioning will gradually be acquired. In order to function productively the group must learn how to evaluate its own progress. Members must learn to view their individual projects as part of a larger group project. Seeing their research as an integral part of the final product can be highly motivating. They will want to be part of the total plan and to work toward its realization, particularly if they shared in its formulation. Participation makes students feel more responsible for their studies and more closely involved in the group. It is important for students to perceive themselves as really capable of influencing decisions about the goals and curriculum; their participation must not be perfunctory (Bany and Johnson, 1964; Gerard, 1957; Rehage, 1951; Solomon and Oberlander, 1974; Stodgill, 1959; Tanner and Lindgren, 1971; Thelen, 1954).

The first step, therefore, is the students' own selection of subject matter and goals. Following this, projects can be chosen to be carried out by individuals or by two students working together. During the selection of the topic, the chairman (or teacher) must avoid adopting the majority opinion too hastily. Everyone should be able to express his preferences. Cutting off the discussion too early could cause dissatisfaction among group members and inhibit the extent of their participation. (Ways of implementing cooperative planning of learning tasks with pupils are presented in Chapter Four.)

Before engaging in full-scale cooperative planning sessions, preliminary meetings should be held at which students can discuss subjects they would like to study, and they can formulate questions for research. The class records and classifies these subjects. This list later serves as the basis for sessions in which a research plan is actually decided upon. When agreement is reached on a particular research topic, it becomes a kind of contract for which each small group assumes responsibility. In turn, each individual is responsible for research into his subtopic. Small-group study, therefore, entails a considerable amount of individual initiative; merely planning the group goal will not guarantee that individuals know how to proceed with their own tasks. After the groups have accepted their part in the general plan, they should then convene to delegate individual projects and explain concrete procedures, at least at the first stages of research. Since all these steps require discussion, groups with a small number of members are more likely to work efficiently.

A group cannot function effectively without a clear notion of its task. Selecting and defining a project is not a one-time event; clarifying and refining the group's concept of its work may be necessary often during its activities. As work progresses and knowledge and understanding increase, the task may be seen in a new light, and it may be necessary to redefine it. Or perhaps the initial plan was vague and students later acquired the knowledge needed to formulate it more clearly and specifically. (Learning activities can be halted during this redefinition.)

Clarification of the tasks also contributes to the group's cohesiveness. Redefining its goals provides the group with another opportunity to share in explaining it. Furthermore, unanimous agreement on the means for achieving the goal also improves the group's efficiency in dealing with cooperative tasks.

Composing groups. The class character as a whole, the nature of the task, the students' ability to work together as a unit, and the degree of friendliness among members when they join the group are all factors which may influence group composition. If the students have had no prior experience in group work, composition might be on the basis of random selection by the teacher. Sometimes a self-choice method or the use of sociometric information will solve all problems simply. Or several of these methods might be combined with the teacher's judgment about students who are likely to work well together.

Here are some guidelines for composing groups:
1.   Pupils who are to work together in a group should know each other well enough to make communication possible without investing time in "breaking the ice." If this

is not possible, teachers should arrange, before the group meets, special sessions during which the members can get acquainted.

2. Teachers should try to compose groups with students having different personalities and expressive styles. Similarity in thought and behavior does not lead to mutual stimulation in group discussion. Variety of interests and personal styles stimulates the group and provides an abundance of skills and abilities.

3. Pupils should be urged to concentrate on the task, not on each other. Comparisons within the group detract attention from the main goal.

4. Pupils with special learning problems should be integrated into groups which the teacher feels will be most beneficial for them and will help them to take an active part in the task. The right group can give a slow learner confidence that he has a valuable role to play and is accepted as a responsible group member (Collins and Guetzkow, 1964; Schmuck and Schmuck, 1971; Thelen, 1949, 1954).

Setting time schedules. Individual members must coordinate their research so that the final report can be prepared at a prearranged time. Students must learn to judge from experience how much time they need for certain tasks. Group projects can be as short as 30 minutes (it would be hard to accomplish anything in less) or as long as several months, depending upon the topics.

Despite the need for general time limits, uniform and arbitrary time limits should not be imposed on group members, so that they can feel relatively free of time pressure. The amount of time allocated to a task should be based on their own honest assessment of the time they need. Teachers will have to help students be realistic, and will probably have to persuade them to take *more* time than they will tend to allot themselves. Scheduling its own group efforts is important for mature group functioning.

Some teachers argue that they can teach students in much less time than that required for them to learn independently, particularly when groups begin to struggle with their organizational needs. There are, of course, situations where direct assistance from the teacher can help a great deal without depriving pupils of their initiative. When the goal is very clear and each one knows the procedures necessary for reaching it, the teacher can probably intervene without affecting group motivation. Or, if the goal is a very concrete one, direct guidance can improve the quality of learning and at the same time actually raise morale. For example, when putting on a play, the assistance of a teacher or director is willingly sought after, without loss of individual involvement or initiative. In research groups, however, it is better for the teacher to assist pupils to plan their own work than to direct the planning himself or herself. The time used for solving group problems is well spent if groups go on to accomplish the goals they set themselves.

After the goal has been decided on and the problem becomes one of procedures, the teacher may ask nondirective questions ("What do you think is necessary as a first step in moving toward this goal?" "How much time do you think is needed to carry out that activity?"). He or she may make time-saving suggestions, as long as these are not taken as regulations which *must* be obeyed. Students will generally want reassurance from their teacher that their project is feasible. It may also help if the teacher reminds students that decisions taken about the group goal at the planning stage can be revised later in the light of their experience.

Group Leadership

Introduction. Without leadership there is no focal point for the organization of a number of people into a group (Gibb, 1947). The group chairman should be an organizing force which enables the group to progress. The teacher is unquestionably the most salient and powerful leader in the classroom. But we will deal here only with the *student* as a leader in the classroom where learning is student-directed (Gibb, 1951; Gordon, 1955; Hare, 1962; Johnson, 1970; Schmuck and Schmuck, 1971; Shaw, 1971).

Who can be chairman? Leaders are developed, not born. In other words, no specific personality is necessary to function as group leader. Leadership consists of a *set of activities* which assist the group in reaching its objectives. *It is a dynamic process reflected in the activities of different group members.* It is *not* the sole prerogative of any one member, nor of the teacher. Each situation demands a unique kind of leadership, and widely different personalities are capable of leading a group.

Small-group teaching creates opportunities for each student to organize and lead group activities, to know that he can influence his classmates and is not without power or status in the group. This knowledge makes him more contented, helps him to identify with the group, and encourages academic achievement. When this feeling is prevalent, the group is productive and makes better progress toward accomplishing its goals. Teachers can help groups to reach this stage of development by ensuring that leadership is equitably distributed among all members (Anderson and Kell, 1954; Cogan, 1958; Lott and Lott, 1966; Schmuck, 1963, 1966; Schmuck and Schmuck, 1971).

When a student takes on the responsibility of leadership, the experience serves as a precedent and he is likely to undertake the job again, particularly if he was successful the first time, in which case he will expect to be so again (Hemphill, 1961). It is important for teachers to help students in leadership positions toward success, in order to enhance group cohesiveness.

Leadership should be rotated and not concentrated in a few students only. Superior verbal expression and persuasive power, or special knowledge which can be used to benefit the group, will doubtlessly make some students stand out as candidates for leadership. Nevertheless, in democratically run groups, all members participate in determining goals and procedures. In addition to the student chosen to serve as chairman for a specified period, others should assume necessary leadership roles (Gordon, 1955; Gulley, 1968). Small-group learning does not claim that all students in a classroom enjoy equal social status, but it does strive to allocate positions of leadership to several students, so that each feels he has some social power and status in his group.

The chairman's role. The chairman's role is to keep the group intact and working toward its goal (Homans, 1950; Johnson, 1970). To do so, he must pay attention to relationships among members which influence the group's survival as a unit. He must know how to help group members to cooperate, but he must likewise be task-oriented.

Two distinct types of group leadership have been described. In both, the chairman seeks to advance the group's progress toward its goal, but one type focuses on the group goal as a way to improve personal relations within the group. The second seeks to improve personal relations mainly as a means of helping the group achieve its goal (Fiedler, 1967). Teachers can direct students' attention to both aspects of the chairman's role, and should also think about whether they themselves are over-engrossed in one particular dimension of their role as class leader.

The chairman's duties comprise three roles. The first is administrative: he delegates roles and/or speaking rights to participants, and tries to resolve conflicts. He should prepare for this task by asking students relevant preparatory questions in advance of the discussion, such as if they have the necessary information, how much time they need to present their ideas, and whether one session will suffice for their presentation. With this information in hand, he can plan the meeting to serve the group's larger goals. When planning how to lead the discussion, it is his duty to consider the entire situation, of which the discussion is only part (Homans, 1950).

The second role is social: the chairman influences relationships in the group. He must safeguard group cohesiveness and develop cooperative potential. When group members feel that their contributions are acceptable and valuable, and that they enjoy full rights of self-expression, cohesiveness will be strengthened and all members can talk freely without worrying about their status in the group. Individual viewpoints are one of the main resources of the group. The chairman should therefore withstand pressure to reach a decision before all the members have had a chance to discuss the issue. He can encourage the presentation of individual views regardless of whether they agree with the majority opinion, and in this way can resist the pressure for conformity so frequently found in groups (Kiesler and Kiesler, 1970). Groups whose chairmen permit free expression to a dissenting minority solve their problems more satisfactorily and more frequently than those in which minority opinion is silenced (Collins and Guetzkow, 1964; Davis, 1969; Maier and Solem, 1952). Other social roles performed by the chairman are to listen to each speaker; to have patience for slow or hesitant speakers; to allow members to be silent if they choose; and to consider *all* the views expressed when the time comes to summarize the presentations.

The third role of the chairman is operational: he sets the entire direction of the group's work in his opening statement, presenting the goal in clear and concrete form. From here he moves to a short presentation of the goal's background. If the project is one requiring discussion rather than research, his opening remarks should stimulate discussion. He must prepare the appropriate questions in advance, and they must not be so vague or difficult as to stifle lively debate. More complex questions can be introduced when the group feels it has the required information. The chairman should restrict speakers' comments to the topic without antagonizing them. If a new topic of discussion is generally considered to be of interest to the group, a subcommittee can be set up to explore it and report to the group at a later date. But irrelevant comments should be kept to a minimum. One way of helping everyone keep to the topic is to summarize the previous discussion and ask a relevant question which still needs clarification, or request speakers to clarify their statements. In groups which tackle problems successfully, members frequently ask each other for information and clarification (Collins and Guetzkow, 1964). At the end of the discussion, or after the meeting at which students combine the results of their individual work, the chairman leads group members in preparing a final report or summarizing the group's decisions.

No one student can be expected to perform successfully *all* of the aspects of the chairman's role. It is preferable for several students to be responsible for different tasks of leadership. They will learn that leadership is not an unattainable quality monopolized by certain people; it is a quality which all students can learn.

Dealing with failures in group functioning. There are a number of potential impediments to effective group functioning. Some critical factors have been discussed in this chapter, such as friendship patterns among group members, group cohesiveness, communication, and the selection of the group task. All of these play an important role in determining whether a group will be able to work together.

When group members can get along and communicate, and when they cooperate on a project which they have all shared in planning and in which they have some interest, discipline problems will be minimal. Keeping groups working toward their own goals is a fundamental aspect of an orderly classroom. Such a classroom will not be a quiet place, indeed it cannot be quiet if it is working to accomplish its goals. But it will be orderly, which means that, despite all the movement and discussion going on, individuals will be involved in pursuing constructive learning tasks.

In order to achieve this end, students must be introduced gradually to group-centered learning. Some may find it difficult to adjust to independent research in cooperation with classmates when they are used to being the recipients of ready-made information dispensed by the teacher. Most students will have to be helped to acquire the skills needed for productive participation in a group. Students may question their ability to work together and thus become easily discouraged. Until they see that group work leads to results, they may not even wish to function as members of a group. Therefore, they must be encouraged to have patience and to improve their group skills so that their experience as group members will be gratifying and productive.

Throughout this book are numerous suggestions for techniques to help students acquire group participation skills. Students must be informed that groups do not function well *automatically*, and that blocks to effective performance are the rule, not the exception. There are many useful techniques to help overcome these blocks, and groups will welcome the opportunity to improve their functioning by practicing the necessary skills which they lack, such as: exercises in cooperative planning; learning how to help each other and to listen to each other (Chapter Four); learning how to increase the measure of agreement between members and spend less time arguing; how to structure discussions so the group can reach conclusions and make decisions (Chapter Five); and learning how to improve relationships among group members through role playing (Chapter Seven).

Teachers can also help students overcome the blocks to effective group work by having students discuss their problems as part of routine group procedures. In these discussions, however, attention must always be focused on the group as a unit and not on individual complaints. Nor should teachers rebuke students accused of infractions or of interfering. In order to facilitate the transition from traditional teaching to group-centered teaching, it is advisable that the students in each group know each other, get along well, and want to work together. If possible, not more than one student should be placed in a group whose other members do not want him as a collaborator. By making groups as cohesive as possible at the start, the transition to group learning will be made with a minimum of conflict and with a reasonable degree of cooperation among students. After students have had experience with this approach, it will be possible to form groups without undue regard for personal preferences, although they will always be honored to some extent.

While these techniques are helpful, problems are always likely to crop up. Teachers anxious about the success of an experiment might reprimand particular pupils, but such behavior only supports the group's scapegoating actions, without improving its ability to cope with problems cooperatively. It would be more advantageous to discuss how the students in question can be integrated into the group so their disorganized behavior will disappear. The group must not be allowed to become a punitive body with power to impose—or instigate—sanctions on its own members. It should rather be led to develop constructive attitudes and techniques, and it should be helped to confront and solve the problems of its own functioning. Problems of human relations must be resolved *within* the group and not by *external* sources of power.

At all times, however, we must bear in mind that small-group teaching seeks to accommodate the variety of individual differences in interest, rate of learning, and ability ordinarily found among students in a classroom. An inability to work in groups can be one of these very differences we wish to accommodate. Not every student can or will work in a group, and those who do not wish to should not be coerced. These students may flourish best with traditional receptive learning, with individualized instruction, or working with one other student only. *It is important that these alternatives be available.*

Group Development

It is unusual for a group to operate efficiently from its beginning. A process of development is generally required until the group learns to deal effectively with problems. Even if the members already know each other, the group has still to clarify its potential, its aims, and its modes of procedure. Students in a newly formed group must learn to cope, for instance, with communication problems or with members who contribute either less or more than their fair share to the group's activities. Only when such obstacles have been overcome can the group function well.

It can be helpful for teachers to recognize some of the typical issues liable to confront a group, since the way the group copes with them reflects its efficiency. If the teacher knows the group's level of development, and hence what kind of behavior to expect from it, he or she is less likely to be discouraged by what seems, superficially, like immaturity and lack of organization. The teacher can then help the group toward greater effectiveness.

Many investigators have described "stages" in group development (Bennis and Shepard, 1956; Hare, 1973; Schmuck and Schmuck, 1974; Schutz, 1958; Tuckman, 1965). Three such stages are discussed below.

Stage One: Developing a sense of belonging and defining goals. It is natural, when we encounter a new environment, to examine it from our own standpoint. It may be a new social environment consisting of people we know only slightly or not at all, and about whom we try to learn more by observing their reaction to others and our own reaction to them. We also try to find out this particular group's accepted norms, its "do's" and "don'ts." At this exploratory stage, we are usually on our best behavior. A friendly and open atmosphere in a group leads to constructive discussion. A formal atmosphere breeds caution and reserve, and although the resulting domination by one or two group members may mean faster decision-making, the decisions are not, in fact, shared equally among the group.

Teachers can help groups toward the necessary skills and cohesiveness by encouraging stimulating discussions and the open expression of ideas. In this uninhibited atmosphere the members will be most likely to work together and to work well. At this stage, the group's main activity is to select and clarify its projects or tasks, and to equitably distribute responsibilities for portions of the work among its members.

Stage Two: Planning procedures and increasing involvement. The development of cooperation brings with it a sense of belonging and of group identity. Desirable as this is for the collective goal, it may threaten individuality and cause some friction among members with differing viewpoints. Any doubts or reservations should be discussed openly so that the students can learn how to combine their own and the group's interests, and thereby function more satisfactorily.

To insure participation by all members, it is important that, at this stage, the decision-making process be defined. Not only the "what's" but the "how's" of the group's aims must be determined, and the working plan must be feasible and acceptable to everyone. Having a clear outcome in sight will encourage members to participate wholeheartedly. The ideal cooperative balance is in itself a goal, and in order to achieve it teachers can help group members to communicate well, to function in different roles, and to evaluate their own progress. Self-evaluation by the group of its own progress can be accomplished, for example, by appointing observers who report to the group on its performance during any specific session (see Chapter Five).

Stage Three: Realizing objectives. When the members feel they belong to a body with an identity and have learned to operate productively, then they are ready to accept both individual and collective responsibility for the group's task. They should all be ready to cooperate with the chairman, whose task is now ideally one of coordinating the members' contributions. At this stage, the bulk of the group's work is carried out.

Teachers should not anticipate too high a degree of efficiency and agreement. A margin must always be allowed for human failings. But even so, a great deal can be accomplished, and there will be a stimulating environment for discussion and investigation.

Once internal and organizational problems have been resolved, most groups will find a reasonably productive level at which to work. Self-evaluation (as suggested above), open discussion of views, and regular checks on the group's progress by the group itself—in conjunction with the teacher—will all help to keep the group on its course.

The transition from one stage of development to another is neither clear-cut nor final, nor is the students' behavior at any one time typical only of that stage. Development is actually a fluid and continuous process, and the group may work at a higher rate of efficiency at some times than at others. The real purpose of dividing the group's progress into "stages" is to help the teacher in his or her observations. Just as developmental level is taken into consideration when assessing a child's accomplishments, so must it be considered when trying to understand a group's performance.

Not every group will reach optimum efficiency. Energy and effort may be wasted on pointless argument or rivalry; but if these are treated as serious topics worthy of discussion, then, with the teacher's help, the group can mature. If successfully undertaken, the resolution of relationships within the group may itself be an experience of major importance to each student's school and future careers.

Chapter Three

Types of Small Groups

The types of small groups discussed here are appropriate for studying the more complex aspects of subjects. They are research groups, discussion groups, groups in learning centers, and gaming groups. There are, of course, many other types of group structures which the teacher can use or invent for teaching different subjects. Once the teacher is accustomed to teaching in groups, he or she is more likely to be innovative in their use. Students, too, can suggest alternative ways of organizing their groups after they have gained experience in group techniques. They will want to suit the kind of group to the task they have chosen.

The Research Group

The aim of the research group is to develop research skills and critical thinking, an approach which can heighten students' sense of responsibility for their studies and help them work independently of the teacher. The research group is one of the teacher's main organizational tools for encouraging students to seek knowledge actively, instead of merely consuming it ready-made. The flexible framework of this kind of group also gives students valuable and realistic experience in cooperative planning and learning. There are many different kinds of research groups, three of which are described here: the equal-roles group (the basic form of research group), the assigned-roles group, and the assigned-opinions group. (Chapter Four presents details of planning projects in research groups.)

Equal-roles group. In this type of group each student is allocated a period of time in which to investigate thoroughly a particular subdivision of the general topic. After all the independent research is complete, the group meets to combine the individual products into a final group report to be presented to the whole class or any other body. In order to do so, each member learns what the others have discovered in their work, and together, the group synthesizes the separate contributions. (A chairman is usually elected to coordinate this process.) During the course of a year the class will build up a small library of reports on all the subjects investigated. An entire year can be spent studying related topics which come under one general heading, in which case the class library can ultimately cover that subject very thoroughly.

Figure 1 depicts this kind of research group.

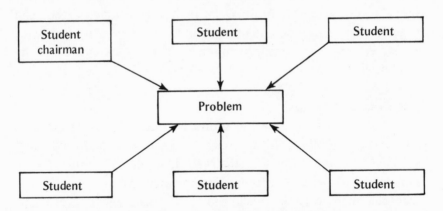

Figure 1. Equal-roles group.

Assigned-roles group. In addition to the basic task of doing research on his chosen sub-topic, each student chooses, or is assigned, an administrative role in the group. In the group described in Figure 2, there are only four members, but the group size may be increased to eight, and the special roles rotated from time to time to ensure the involvement of each student and to avoid domination by any one individual. Some of the typical responsibilities of each task are as follows (Institute for Development of Educational Activities, 1971):

Chairman. The chairman's main job is to help the group achieve its goal. After members have gathered the necessary data, the chairman and secretary may cooperate in preparing the final report for presentation to the entire class. If necessary, the chairman's post can be filled by two students—one supervising group interactions (such as directing the flow of communication and reducing any tensions which might restrict discussion), and the second concentrating on the content of the discussion to ensure that comments are confined to the subject and that the discussion progresses and is not repetitious.

Technician. The person occupying this post should be aware of the group's goal in relation to the research plan of the whole class. He should be able to call the group's attention to irrelevancy in its activities, though to do so might require further clarification of the goal.

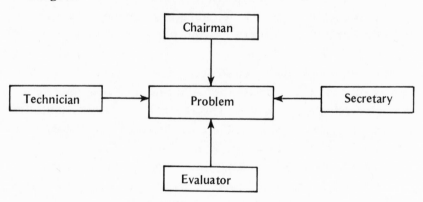

Figure 2. Assigned-roles group.

Secretary. The secretary must keep a detailed record of the group's discussions and decisions, and can request additional clarification of vague statements or unsupported claims. He may serve as spokesman for the group when reporting its results to some larger body (other groups, the entire class, several classes, or the entire school).

Evaluator. Information gathered by each member must be distributed to the whole group, and this is the task of the evaluator. He also evaluates the relevancy of this information to the goal and its place in material being prepared by the group. The evaluator should not express opinions about the quality of the work done by other members, nor should he give grades or compare students' work. In fact, no grades or comparative values are awarded to individuals. Evaluation must focus exclusively on the cooperative group products.

All the chairmen, technicians, secretaries, and evaluators from the various groups can meet with the teacher before and during the research effort to clarify their roles or to discuss other problems which arise. Afterwards, they return to their original groups.

Assigned-opinions group. In this kind of group a point of view is assigned to or chosen by each group member, and his job is to investigate this position in relation to the problem under study (an approach similar to that of formal debating teams, where the point of view to be defended is decided in advance). The decision to present a particular position does not need to bear any relation to the individual's own beliefs. This is a marvelous opportunity for students to learn to see someone else's perspective and argue that position objectively. See Figure 3.

Teachers may wish to assign the investigation of a particular opinion to an entire group. Several groups would then investigate the same issue, each from a different point of view.

In research groups, however, no debate is necessary, although the stage of gathering information about a topic could be a preparatory step for a debate to be conducted between different research groups. The topic under study must obviously arouse

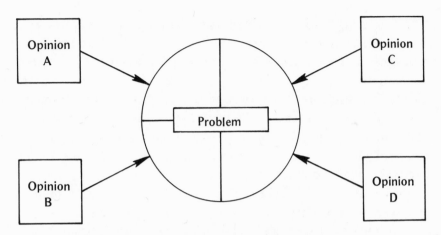

Figure 3. Assigned-opinions group.

some controversy if it is to stimulate students to investigate differing points of view; thus, if it has a clear, simple solution, it is not appropriate for this kind of study. Teachers can even assist groups to reach the discussion stage rapidly by actually supplying all the necessary material. One fact-sheet might sometimes suffice to provide all data required as the basis for discussion. This approach is particularly valuable if the students are to concentrate on the intellectual implications of the subject rather than on fact-finding.

Teachers can help students develop the skills needed for independent research, which may mean helping them learn how to use reference books in the school or public library; how to use different sources for their information; how to compile a bibliography; how to organize and classify information logically; and how to analyze and evaluate their information. Orderly and meaningful presentation of the results of their research is another skill that teachers can help develop in their pupils; it is gratifying for them to see the fruits of their efforts. By helping students when necessary, teachers can make independent and cooperative learning experiences possible for them without handing them ready-made information.

Gathering information will sometimes require visits to local universities, libraries, industry, or government institutions. Students may interview people in the community and make site visits. To be both accurate and realistic, active searching for data should ideally lead students to a variety of sources. The day of the single textbook is over, at least as the total diet on any subject. Through research groups pupils can learn that knowledge is a complex weave of ideas and facts and an integral part of life, not something irrelevant, acquired in school.

The approach of research groups emphasizes critical thinking and systematic investigation. Group learning activities should be defined by logical steps and procedures characteristic of scientific research, which may be described as follows:

(1) formulating the problem or goal;
(2) formulating a hypothesis about the possible expected results;
(3) planning the practical procedures of the research;
(4) executing the study according to these formulations;
(5) interpreting data gathered during step 4; and
(6) synthesizing all the findings obtained in the study.

The Discussion Group

The active involvement of every student in discussing the topic is the goal of the discussion group. It strives to develop basic skills required for the orderly conduct of a discussion, such as speaking in turn, listening to others, and confining remarks to the topic. Discussion helps pupils to clarify their own ideas and helps them become aware of others' opinions. The structure of a discussion group might look something like Figure 4.

The group in Figure 4 comprises five members, but similar groups can function with between two and eight. Teachers should severely limit their own participation in discussion groups. Their role should be to advise pupils how to fulfill their tasks independently. Students themselves must make sure that everyone

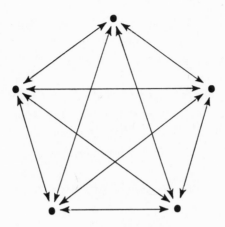

*Figure 4. Communication channels in
a discussion group.*

in the group can express himself without fear or inhibition. Constructive group discussion could produce a better solution to the problem than that of any single member.

Discussion groups also require a chairman, whose task is to introduce the topic and supervise the discussion in a friendly way. The chairman may ask the speakers questions to clarify their comments, try to synthesize speakers' concepts, and ensure that the discussion progresses, though he must be cautious not to monopolize it or to use his position to the disadvantage of other participants. The discussion is usually summarized by someone other than the chairman.

The discussion topic may be determined by the curriculum or selected from current world or local events or other sources, in accordance with the students' decisions. After it has been chosen, a list should be made of specific questions which the discussion should try to answer. (How to conduct a group discussion is the topic of Chapter Five.)

Learning Centers
Learning centers are any area in or near the classroom where

learning materials are placed so they can be used freely by pupils. Learning centers provide a certain type of learning environment for student groups, enabling them to choose their subject matter from several alternatives, since a variety of centers is usually available. It also introduces individual approaches to learning, in terms of pace and content, while still allowing students to cooperate. They are not obliged to work alone if they prefer to work with others; the decision should be theirs.

Figure 5. Groups in learning centers.

Even if the subject matter from a learning center is chosen by the teacher, students should have some measure of choice in selecting which center to use, or in deciding to change from one to another after a time. Involvement in the actual planning and construction of learning centers is even more motivating for them (Baker, Ross, and Walters, 1971; Cote and Gurske, 1970; Hertzberg and Stone, 1971; Voight, 1971). (Chapter Six deals with how to organize learning centers in the classroom.)

Learning Through Group Play

Learning is traditionally regarded as "work," and play, relegated to the playground, is not usually considered an integral part of it. Today, however, play is recognized as an important and effective medium for learning. People of all ages and cultures learn through games and *enjoy it*. The fun aspect, often lacking in other forms of learning, makes a vital contribution to intellectual and emotional growth (Boocock, 1968; Herron and Sutton-Smith, 1971).

It is worth noting that most games take place in a small group. If a large group is involved, it usually consists of spectators, not players. The players must interact with one another and be constantly involved in the task—both actions which are facilitated by small groups but restricted by large ones. This fact has long been recognized in drama and sport, and education can also benefit from it.

Educators have long acknowledged the positive effect of a play atmosphere on pupils' willingness to study materials that might otherwise be tedious. Games have been devised to improve specific learning skills, but with their emphasis on the mastery of skills or facts, they are directed at individuals, not groups. Their social features are secondary, unlike role playing and simulation games, in which the social context is an important component.

Role playing is a form of drama in which the spontaneous acting roles allow students to create and become directly involved in human relations. The fact that the dramatic situation is "make believe" helps participants to express themselves uninhibitedly (Hendry, Lippitt, and Zander, 1947; Klein, 1959; Schmuck and Schmuck, 1971). Simulation games seek to represent complex social systems involving various groups of people and help the players understand and analyze the situation (Abt, 1968; Boocock, 1968; Gordon, 1970; Inbar and Stoll, 1972; Nesbitt, 1971). (Details of these processes are dealt with in Chapters Seven and Eight.)

There are educational games which may not qualify as simulation games, but whose aim is more than simply mastering skills. One example—there are many, of course—is "Twenty

Questions," which can cover intellectual problems on any kind of subject and in which children of almost any age (above kindergarten) can take part. The original television game was played by a "panel of experts" who were allowed a maximum of 20 questions in which to find the answer to something very specific, such as identifying the examinee's occupation. In an educational setting the game can be changed to be more instructive, and, as 20 questions are inadequate to explore a topic seriously, the number should be increased to at least 30 (Taylor and Faust, 1952).

"Thirty Questions" uses the same strategy as the television game, namely, solving a problem by interrogating an "expert" on the subject, or whichever person knows the solution. Four students make up the panel of interrogators. Although the game appears superficially simple, considerable time and effort are required for background preparation. One group of students is responsible for research into and formulation of the actual problem. The members must consider seriously the questions they expect will be asked, in order to conduct their research thoroughly. They must then inform the "expert" so that he is fully prepared to answer the panel's questions accurately. Naturally, their decisions and preparations must be kept strictly secret. At the same time, the panel can decide upon its questioning strategy. This game differs from its television counterpart in that the problem is not presented to the panel suddenly; it should be announced well in advance so that the panel can prepare its questions. This game is something between a courtroom cross-examination and a group guessing game, and can be an intriguing educational experience with much intellectual stimulation. It also allows panel members to confer freely and benefit from a cooperative group effort. The panel should always retain its group character, so there must be enough time for members to confer often.

The examinee may also need to consult his committee. He may reply to questions only with yes or no. A comment such as "that's partially correct," or "not in the ordinary sense of the word," can also be permitted. He may ask the examiner to rephrase his question. This game will only be gratifying to students if it follows a period of careful preparation. Knowing that their own research has prepared them fully for the game, students will feel more actively involved and will analyze the issues under investigation carefully. In a large class, several such games could be played simultaneously, each involving three groups (two committees and a group of spectators).

Combining Different Kinds of Groups for Learning

All the techniques described in the following chapters are intended to involve students actively in learning as group members. Group membership requires productive communication, cooperation, and regulation of the students' learning pace. It also places emphasis on critical analysis as an important part of the educational process.

It is important to remember that the distinction between one kind of group and another is often quite arbitrary. The groups are presented here as separate entities only for the sake of clarity; in practice, it might be unnecessary to distinguish between them. Even when a group is formed for a specific purpose, it can quickly merge into a different kind of unit. For example, a research group might be set up to investigate a given subject. After the initial work is completed, the group wants to discuss the individuals' findings before going into further research. The research group then becomes a discussion group, which operates in a different way. The discussion continues until all the information has been clarified and the group decides to return to its research activities. The members may decide to act out certain ideas in role playing in order to improve understanding of what they are investigating, so once again the group alters its structure, while continuing to pursue its original goal.

Different kinds of groups can and should be used in conjunction with one another. Role playing and simulation games (see Chapters Seven and Eight), for example, are best employed as part of an overall group approach to classroom organization, rather than as individual and isolated techniques. The techniques discussed here are related and complementary. Using them together can also avoid repetition of the same technique. For example, in a class study of "A Walk on the Moon," separate research groups could be formed to investigate various aspects, such as the clothing needed by astronauts, food and oxygen supply, and transportation to and on the moon; each group could report its findings to the entire class.

Groups can find their information in many ways. Some may use special learning centers set up in the classroom for this purpose (see Chapter Six). After facts have been assembled, distributed, and analyzed, the subject may be debated in a broader context (see Chapter Five). Possible topics for discussion could be the need for international agreements on the control of space, supervision of the moon's surface as a scientific site, or changes in man's self-image resulting from the moon landing. When the issues have been thoroughly discussed, the class can compose and act out a simulation game covering some of the critical problems involved in getting to and walking on the moon, including the complex preparations (see Chapter Eight). The game is certain to uncover new problems and thereby stimulate further study.

Successful use of these techniques requires only the normal equipment and materials found in the average classroom. The emphasis is on the social organization of the students and a restructuring of both the students' and teacher's roles, rather than on new and/or expensive instructional media and material.

While the various types of group structures can be employed singly or in conjunction with each other, they are not all equally effective at all age levels. Learning centers are used more often in the lower elementary grades, and simulation games from the middle elementary grades and up but particularly in high school and college. However, learning centers could be used creatively even with older groups, especially when planned by the students themselves, such as when a group wishes to report to classmates about its research activities. Group discussions certainly can and should be conducted in the lower elementary grades, but, in general, they become more intellectually productive as one moves up the age scale. On the other hand, cooperative planning groups and buzz groups (see Chapter Four), various kinds of research groups, and role playing are used effectively at all levels of elementary and secondary school as well as in universities.

Teachers will have to help students select the type of group structure or learning strategy best suited to their needs for the task at hand. By being aware of the many alternatives available, teachers can help students organize themselves efficiently. Using his or her knowledge of the students' abilities, interests, and goals to judge which type of group structure is most appropriate for given tasks constitutes one of the teacher's major roles as guide and catalyst in learning.

Chapter Four

Organizing Small-Group Learning

To implement the principles of grouping in the classroom, the teacher must ensure that he or she and the pupils acquire skills necessary for working in groups. The lack of these skills can often frustrate the pupils' and the teacher's desire to work cooperatively (Stanford and Roark, 1974). The necessary skills can be specifically practiced as part of the transition to group learning. Pupils need help in learning how to plan their work cooperatively, how to lead a group, and how to listen to each other. This chapter will deal with the transition to small group learning and with the rudiments of cooperative planning. Chapter Five presents discussion skills required for working together in small groups. (For a detailed exposition of the development of communication in groups, see Stanford and Roark, 1974.)

TRANSITION

The transition from traditional one-group teaching to the classroom where several small groups function simultaneously is best accomplished gradually. Both teacher and pupils can practice the necessary skills and evaluate their effectiveness in a variety of ways, some of which are described below.

Initial Steps for Subdividing Classes

As an initial step, a group of three or four students can deal with one particular task, while the rest of the class continues to study in the usual way (Miel, 1952). This small group operates on behalf of the class and ultimately will present the results of its work to the class. Selection of the small-group members by the class, rather than by the teacher, ensures that the other students will view the group as representatives of the entire class.

Topics can, of course, be investigated at various levels of complexity according to the age of the students, but here are some suggestions for activities one group can carry out:

1. Visit a school, library, factory, hospital, laboratory, university, or similar institution, after which the group reports its experience to the class. This task is appropriate when it is impossible for the entire class to make the trip.

2. Choose a play to be performed by the class or present a list of plays from which the class can choose.

3. Write a joint letter to a sick classmate.

4. Prepare a class party. The group can organize details itself or decide on procedures and distribute tasks to other classmates.

5. Plan decorations for the party.

6. Plan a trip for the whole class.

7. Conduct interviews with personalities such as city government officials, school board members, police representatives, leaders of local political organizations, or ethnic group representatives.

This technique can be used to subdivide an entire class into several small groups, so that every child in the class has a chance to participate in a small short-term group. The group task should be relatively easy, and all the groups, working simultaneously, should be able to complete their projects in an hour or two. In this way the teacher can initiate small-group activities without drastically changing the usual routine or social structure of the class. The groups could plan a game for a class party, or prepare a different task, such as planning an interview, writing a critique of a newspaper editorial, or conducting a short scientific experiment.

All of these projects involve the students in the productive procedures of clarifying their goal and specifying the methods of achieving it. The group must distribute tasks evenly, consider time factors, and survey its resources. Even at this early "warming-up" stage, they may feel the need to elect a chairman to direct the discussion. In each case the group must report its results to the class. It is also advisable to devote time to a discussion (possibly with the entire class) of the research and study procedures used by the groups. This will also help the transition to small-group learning.

Buzz Groups

Buzz groups can ease the transition to small-group structure in the class and are also an efficient tool to enable pupils to voice their reactions to topics or specific events. They comprise small groups which meet for a few minutes, freeing pupils from "stage fright," which often inhibits their contribution to large-group discussions (Gorman, 1969; Leypoldt, 1967). The class is divided into four- or six-person groups whose goal is to clarify a carefully limited problem, answer specific questions, or encourage each pupil to express an opinion on a given subject. The issues are to be raised later at a class meeting, so buzz-group meetings generally serve as preliminary discussions in preparation for a more detailed discussion (Thelen, 1954).

Here are the steps for forming and using buzz groups:

1. Pupils and teacher outline the problem to be discussed by all groups. This could stem from the subject matter already being studied (for example: what are the forces which led to the outbreak of a particular war?); or the class could analyze the growth of social relations in the classroom; or plan a project with a view to stimulating social contact among pupils (such as a play, picnic, or a party).

2. The class is divided into small groups. Each group chooses a secretary, who records all the members' suggestions and, of course, joins in the discussion himself.

3. The average length of a meeting is ten minutes. The teacher gives a five-minute warning before time is up, and a signal for ending the session. During the session the teacher moves among the groups to see that all students are participating.

4. The groups convene and each secretary reports on his group's suggestions for dealing with the issue.

5. The chairman (or the teacher acting as chairman) may ask for additional comments from students, and then summarizes the reports given by all the secretaries.

6. Additional discussion may be necessary, or the class may be able to decide its course of action in the light of the suggestions already offered.

Buzz groups are appropriate in any grade, and are even an effective learning device in the lower grades, as illustrated in the following example.

In one second-grade project, the classroom was called "Satellite City" and divided into several "neighborhoods": an agricultural area, a section of public parks, and an industrial zone where rockets were manufactured. A large mural depicted the entire town and was later referred to frequently when pupils were explaining their particular positions. All major issues were to be presented to the town council. Small groups of pupils, representing neighborhoods and communities with special interests, met in buzz groups to clarify their positions in preparation for a council meeting, at which all the groups presented their cases.

One day the teacher confronted the town with a problem; a rocket manufacturer requested a permit from the town council to purchase additional land on which to build a launching pad. The land was now part of the public park area. Pupils were divided into groups representing neighborhoods and special interests (such as a parks committee, farmers, homeowners, and the rocket industry). In ten-minute buzz sessions they discussed their reactions to the request while the secretaries recorded their comments.

A town council meeting followed, at which the council sat in a semi-circle at the head of the class and each secretary presented his group's position. The council asked several questions the secretaries could not answer, so a short recess was called for groups to hold another buzz session to deal with the unanswered problems; then the council meeting was reconvened. Certain points made by secretaries about the effects of rocket-launching on their particular zone were illustrated clearly by reference to the large plan of the town.

After hearing all the arguments, the council called its own meeting, where only council members were allowed to speak. The evidence was discussed and a vote was taken to decide whether the manufacturer could purchase the land for the purpose stated. The teacher collected and edited the notes from all the secretaries, added the minutes of the council meeting, mimeographed them, and gave each pupil a copy.

Developing Skills for Participation
in Small Groups

In order to study effectively in small groups, students must be helped to acquire the skills and functions requisite for group participation or leadership. Baker, Smith, Walters, and Wetzel (1971) developed a series of practice lessons for the lower grades of elementary school with this aim. The fundamental skills they include are:

- Reading instructions to the group and answering questions about the assignment.
- Distributing and sharing the materials needed for the assignment, and cleaning up the work area.
- Mutual help.

- Evaluating the group activity.

Prior to conducting the four small-group lessons, the teacher and the *entire class* discuss the benefits of small-group work. The teacher writes down the students' ideas on a chart, which may include the following suggestions:

- Students can help each other.
- They can learn from each other.
- They can learn to be independent (learn without a teacher).
- The teacher can help more by working with one small group at a time while other groups work independently.

The teacher should explain the reasons for having a leader in each group and the need for written instructions. He or she should also praise appropriate behavior; the remarks should be specific, such as: "This group has so many ideas. Marie and Peter asked such good questions, and Johnny and Joe are listening attentively."

The following four lessons are devoted to putting into practice the skills outlined above. Before each lesson the entire class reviews the skills learned in the previous lesson. Afterwards the teacher conducts the practice lesson with one small group at a time, while the rest of the students work at individual assignments. Each group consists of five or six students and the teacher. First they discuss the value of the skills to be learned. The teacher lists the skills on a chart using the students' own words. The pupils then practice the skills in turn.

The teacher demonstrates the kinds of behavior to be learned and again praises good performance accordingly. Praise must be specific.

At the end of each practice lesson the group evaluates its performance and decides whether the members did in fact learn the skills they set out to learn. Here is an outline of the four practice lessons:

Lesson I. Reading and understanding instructions.

1.   General review of the reasons for forming the class into small groups. The rest of the lesson is conducted with one small group at a time.

2.   Materials. The teacher should prepare four or five charts with samples of instructions and activity cards or work sheets, which are appropriate for use in learning centers (see Chapter Six). A practice chart for the second grade may include instructions such as:

   a.   Make a map of the classroom.
   b.   How wide is our room? Count your steps.
   c.   How long is our room? Count your steps.
   d.   Draw our room on your graph paper.
   e.   Add details (desks, sink, windows).

   The teacher also needs a large piece of paper or tagboard on which to write down lesson objectives.

3.   Methods for accomplishing the objectives.

   a.   The group first discusses why it needs written instructions (for example, they are a substitute for direct teacher guidance). The teacher then leads the group in a short discussion of how the instructions are to be read and by whom, and suggests that group members should listen quietly while the instructions are being read. He or she makes a chart of the objectives of the lesson:
      (1)   Read instructions aloud.
      (2)   Listen carefully.
      (3)   Ask questions when you don't understand.
      (4)   Answer questions and explain instructions.

   b.   The teacher demonstrates the objectives by playing the part of leader and reading the instructions aloud. The children then take turns reading instructions from any one of the prepared charts.

   c.   Throughout the lesson the teacher encourages appropriate behavior, which, in this lesson, means reading instructions loudly and clearly, asking the group for questions, listening quietly, and participating in the discussion.

d.   The group determines whether or not the children learned the skills defined as the goals of the lesson.

Lesson II. Distributing materials and cleaning up the work area.

1.   General review of the previous lesson. The rest of Lesson II is conducted with one small group at a time.

2.   Materials. The teacher prepares four or five sets of materials suitable for group activities in any subject (math, art, language, etc.) and a chart to record the objectives of the lesson.

3.   Methods for accomplishing the objectives.

a.   The group discusses the procedures to be carried out after the instructions are read by the leader. The teacher lists the procedures on his or her chart.

(1)   Distribute materials.

(2)   Leader is to be provided with any additional materials needed.

(3)   Group members share materials.

(4)   Group members clean up work area.

(5)   Everyone puts complete work away.

b.   The teacher first demonstrates how to pass out materials and clean up the work area. Each student in turn then practices the role of leader. He passes around materials and gets any other materials the group might need. All group members practice sharing materials and putting away the finished work.

c.   Throughout the session the teacher again backs appropriate behavior with specific praise, such as: "It was very helpful of John to hand the scissors to Jim when he was finished." "This group is doing a good job of putting the materials away."

    d.   The group discusses whether it has learned to carry out all of the procedures listed on the chart of objectives.

Lesson III. Helping each other.

1.   General review of previous lessons. It is again helpful for the teacher to praise the students for what they have learned and for considerate group behavior.

2.   Materials. The group uses the charts prepared for the second lesson (with samples of instructions). The teacher prepares necessary materials and chart paper for writing down the objectives of this lesson.

3.   Methods for accomplishing the objectives.

    a.   First the group discusses how the leader can determine whether a particular group member needs help, how members can help each other, and whether they should criticize each other. The teacher writes down the objectives of the lesson:

        (1)   Leader should ask if anyone needs help.

        (2)   Group members help each other.

        (3)   Group members praise each other.

    b.   The teacher demonstrates the required behavior by reading the instructions loudly and clearly, handing out the materials, asking for questions, providing help where necessary, and praising all appropriate behavior. To complete all of the instructions at the start would probably be too time-consuming.

    c.   The students practice the behaviors stressed in this lesson. Each should have a chance to be a leader and ask others if they need help. In addition, group members help each other and praise each other's good behavior.

    d.   The teacher should encourage the students to praise each other, as they may not previously have been accustomed to doing so. He or she could ask such questions as: "Can we think of something nice to say to

Judy for being such a good leader?" or "What can we say when someone does something we like?"

e.   Once again the teacher offers specific praise, such as "Jim, it was good of you to remember to ask if anyone needed help."

f.   The group discusses whether they have accomplished the objectives listed on the chart (see section 3a of this lesson).

Lesson IV. Evaluating the group activity.

1.   General review of previous lessons. The class may refer to all the charts. It divides into small groups for the rest of this lesson.

2.   The teacher prepares chart paper for listing the objectives of this lesson. He or she also presents each group with a checklist of the objectives taught throughout the five lessons, which may look something like this:

"Group Members" and Group Leader's Checklist

Yes	No	1. Were the instructions read aloud?
Yes	No	2. Did everybody listen to the instructions?
Yes	No	3. Did you pass out materials?
Yes	No	4. Did all members help each other?
Yes	No	5. Did all members praise each other?
Yes	No	6. Did everybody clean up?
Yes	No	7. Did everybody discuss the lesson?

Date ....   Leader's Name........................

3.   Methods for accomplishing the objectives.

a.   The group discusses how to judge whether the group activity was successful. The teacher lists the objectives of this lesson on chart paper:

(1)   Leader will ask group to talk about activity.

(2)   Group members will talk about the activity.

(3)   Leader will fill out the checklist with the help of the group.

b.   The teacher should demonstrate how to fill out the checklist. The group may base the evaluation on all the activities carried out during the training program. The teacher may say: "Now that we have finished our activity, let's decide if it was successful." He or she reads each item on the checklist and discusses it with the group. The members decide whether each objective was fulfilled. If there is disagreement, a vote can be taken.

4.   Every student gets a chance to practice the role of leader. He reads each item on the checklist and asks the group whether the answer should be yes or no.

5.   During the entire lesson the teacher again praises good group behavior, such as listening attentively, asking questions, participating in the discussion, or simply sitting quietly.

6.   The group evaluates the lesson by discussing its performance. Did each student lead the group discussion and evaluate the lesson using the checklist? Did all members participate in the discussion?

By the end of these four lessons every student should have practiced some participation and leadership skills. If the teacher notices that some students have difficulty with some of the skills, a review lesson may be conducted with small groups.

Exercise for Developing Listening Skills

Participation in group activities does not have to be vocal. Another valuable exercise is *creative listening*, in which students evaluate other members' suggestions and express their own opinion only toward the end of the discussion. Listening is not the natural endowment of everyone. We often fail to understand what we hear because we are so immersed in what we are trying to say that we hear only part of what the *other* person is saying.

Small-group work entails extensive discussion, and the pupils' ability to listen well is crucial for effective group membership.

Gorman (1969) proposes the following exercise to improve listening skills by having students check each other's attention to the group discussion:

1. The teacher lists on the blackboard three or four topics of discussion which should be of intrinsic interest to the pupils.

2. The class is divided into groups of three, with group members sitting as far from each other as possible.

3. The teacher explains that each group must choose one of the topics on the board, and allows two or three minutes for the choice to be made.

4. The groups then discuss the topics they chose, according to the following rule: each speaker (except, of course, the first) must summarize the preceding speaker's remarks briefly before beginning his statement. If students think their ideas were not accurately summarized, they must say so.

5. The discussions last about 20 minutes, after which the teacher stops them, and, for three minutes each group discusses how well the members listened to others' statements.

6. The entire class discusses the exercise. The following questions may be used as a guide: Was it difficult to summarize your classmates' remarks? Was the difficulty due to lack of clarity in the statement itself, or to the length of the statement and the number of ideas expressed in it?

7. Each student asks if others had difficulty understanding him. Students should also ask themselves whether they pay as much attention to other people's statements as they did in this exercise.

8. The class discusses ways to improve communication among the students.

Teaching Reading in Groups

Reading can be taught by a variety of teaching methods and is therefore a convenient subject area in which to introduce small-group learning. Reading can be taught to the class as a whole, on an individual basis, or in small groups. By "reading" we mean not merely the teaching of letter or word recognition, but the entire spectrum of reading skills, including word attack skills, comprehension, expressive reading, and reading fluency. Pupils master these skills at different rates, and some may require years of practice. By combining various teaching methods the teacher can deal with every child according to his needs.

One of the main goals of teaching reading in small groups is to maximize teaching efficiency: pupils should be grouped according to their needs, so that those with a particular weakness can be helped together without holding up the rest of the class (Veatch, 1966). The group has a short session with the teacher while their classmates read or engage in whatever pursuits the teacher has previously planned for them.

Even pupils at the first reading stages may be organized into small groups. For example, the entire class could learn a letter and then pupils could divide into groups, one reviewing the lesson with the teacher, a second looking at picture-books, and a third perhaps playing an appropriate reading game.

Keeping individual progress records is an integral part of this teaching method. Meeting with each pupil makes it possible for the teacher to note his progress and difficulties. During the meeting the child reads for the teacher, who records his progress and thus plans future work. These records also serve as a basis for grouping together pupils with similar learning needs. Group and individual instruction are clearly complementary here and should be interchanged as needed.

When a group of this kind is formed, it meets with the teacher for five to ten minutes (which may be the maximum time the teacher can devote to one group). The number of times the group meets, with or without the teacher, depends on how quickly they master the particular skill; it may be one session or many. The teacher may sometimes spend the entire ten minutes helping the group; but at other times the group can be allocated a task by the teacher, and then work independently. In this case group members may help each other and listen to each other read. They disband when everyone has completed the task.

Children may form groups to read aloud to each other. Members of these groups need not have any specific reading problem in common, the reason for their joining being nothing more than interest or friendship. They may want to act various roles in a story, conduct miniature role-playing sessions related to the story, or perhaps read aloud their own stories (Magers, 1968; Perry, 1950; Shaftel and Shaftel, 1967). One or two sessions might be spent writing a play or story around some feature of the book being studied. In this way all aspects of reading can be explored, from a didactic as well as from a creative point of view. At the same time, the participants in these groups experience the rudimentary features of working in groups: communication and cooperation.

Organizing group sessions. The following timetable, allowing one and a half hours for reading activities, is an example of how both individual and group meetings can be arranged.

9:00 a.m.   Students select books they will read that morning. They sit on chairs, on the floor, or in any position they prefer.

9:15 a.m.   The teacher meets with several students individ-
to   ually; their names are on the board when the class
10:00 a.m.   arrives in the morning.

10:00 a.m.   The teacher holds short sessions with "skill groups," whose members have common problems.

Groups might be organized as follows:

10:00 a.m. to 10:15 a.m.	A group with problems in blending.
10:16 a.m. to 10:20 a.m.	A group which needs help in choosing the books it needs on a particular topic.
10:21 a.m. to 10:30 a.m.	Another group practices expressive reading; every pupil reads a few lines aloud, and the teacher emphasizes the feelings expressed in the text. Pupils and teacher together then discuss how these emotions should best be expressed.

Teachers can prepare in advance the appropriate arrangement of chairs in different parts of the room, so that noise made by pupils moving the furniture is kept to a minimum.

The groups described here differ somewhat from those discussed elsewhere in this book. Reading groups do not devote much time or thought to developing communication among members; the groups' aims are rather directed toward mastery of specific learning skills. This multi-method approach to reading does, however, open up a wide variety of learning experiences to students and frees them from lock-step constraints on potential progress.

COOPERATIVE PLANNING

Cooperation in planning group tasks serves to heighten student involvement in the group process. It is a means by which students take active part in determining what they will study and how they will proceed.

Cooperative planning can involve the entire class as well as small groups within the class. In the early stages of selecting a topic of study, the entire class can suggest which aspects of it should be investigated. The large group can also plan how to divide the topic: whether all small groups within the class will sub-sequently investigate the same topic or whether each one will be responsible for a different aspect of the topic. During the course of their work, each small group plans its own specific sub-topic, procedures, resources, and distribution of roles among its members. From time to time the teacher may choose to review the progress of investigation separately with each group or with the class as a whole. At such times, students evaluate their work and, if necessary, modify their plans.

In some classrooms cooperative planning is applied to every side of school life; formulating rules and schedules, taking care of the classroom, and even planning the curriculum (Miel, 1952). The pupils themselves often suggest subjects for group research, which can be as diverse as "What was life like in the country where my grandparents were born?" or "How do airplanes work?" The students' curiosity may be aroused by objects brought to the class, such as books, specimens, or birthday gifts, from which an imaginative teacher can start an intensive investigation. Holidays, seasons, and social or political events are also potential subjects for study of this kind.

Burton (1962) cites an example of a study topic generated by chance events in the classroom. Two fifth-grade students found some rocks and brought them to school to try to identify them. Other pupils then recalled that they had also found some interesting rocks. A display of different stones was eventually made. The students raised many questions about them: why some were hard and others soft; why some were smooth and others rough; what caused some to have color. They compiled a long list of their own questions, which were organized into topics. Then the students each chose a particular topic and, accordingly, formed several small groups, to perform experiments, read books and articles, and build their own rock collections.

Some teachers consider total student participation in planning the curriculum undesirable, but small-group learning is also feasible within a preformulated curriculum. There can still be opportunities for group planning of the learning process, and teachers can arouse pupils' interest in subject matter which the curriculum obliges them to study. Often a curriculum merely defines a general subject area, leaving specific issues for investigation to be determined by teachers and students. Furthermore, most subjects encompass a variety of phenomena of which students should be aware. Visits to sites or museums, films, or plays can reveal some fascinating possibilities for research in any subject area.

A Small-Group Approach to Unit Teaching

Using instructional units as a principal means for teaching subject matter from various perspectives is a fairly widespread technique in the elementary school. Through the units a wide range of subjects, such as science, literature, music, mathematics, and crafts, can be related to each other. A broad instructional unit emphasizes the common points of seemingly diverse topics. It also provides opportunities for practicing basic skills, such as reading, writing, measuring, map reading, or vocabulary development, in a context which integrates the different elements. A variety of activities related to the main motif of the unit can also be introduced, for example, trips, site visits, sculpting, or painting (Burton, 1962; Hanna, Potter, and Hageman, 1961; Stanford and Roark, 1974).

The small-group approach to unit teaching increases student participation without changing the unit's fundamental structure. The group method requires cooperation between pupils and teachers in planning the topic, the instructional goals for each section, and the allocation of roles to groups and group members. The main feature of unit teaching as a group experience, rather than a subject-centered teaching plan, is cooperative planning— among the students as well as between the students and the teacher—instead of exclusive planning by the teacher. In this method, in contrast to traditional teaching concepts, students are involved in the selection of topics to be studied, in decision-making, in the allocation of roles, and in defining learning procedures. Active participation in all the planning stages ensures a sense of involvement in learning.

The unit usually begins when the teacher arranges, in one corner of the room, a display including pictures, maps, books, and objects illustrating different aspects of the general topic. If the subject lends itself to experimentation (such as topics in the natural or biological sciences), the instruments, materials, or specimens also can be displayed.

From the students' reactions to the display, the teacher learns how much they know about the subject. With this information as a basis, a discussion can be held to develop the topic in preparation for group work. In the upper elementary grades, teachers may present topics through class discussion without displaying materials. This discussion is a means for stimulating students' interest and for making notes about their own knowledge of the subject (Hanna, Porter, and Hageman, 1961).

As an alternative to the teacher's introduction to the unit, he or she can help one group of students present the subject to the rest of the class. Three or four students can introduce the unit by one of many activities, such as preparing an appropriate display; visiting a relevant site or institution and reporting to the class; preparing a map which highlights relevant features of the unit; or setting up a learning center with several stimulating tasks.

Cooperative planning. Once students show genuine interest in a subject, they will formulate tentative questions which they might attempt to answer during their investigation. This discussion of probable goals can be the first step in cooperative planning, and it allows students and teachers to raise suggestions about the specific issues to be studied. Some of the suggestions ultimately may be discarded, and the class will focus its efforts on a few chosen problems, which are listed and distributed to all the groups.

The time factor must also be considered in planning. Projects in the first years of elementary school are best planned for periods from a day to a week, or, at the most, two. Even when time limits are set for the overall project, pupils frequently review their goals and the allocation of roles, and group membership and tasks are often changed during the project. For example, in the Satellite City project previously described, pupils met every morning to review their problems or to choose new ones, and then composed groups to deal with them. Although group membership remained fairly stable, pupils were not irrevocably assigned to a particular group, and could move to another if they wished.

In advanced elementary grades and at higher levels, projects may last for one or several months, or even longer. Sometimes classes plan a series of interlocking projects, all related in some way, which constitutes their curriculum for an entire year. In such cases, it is essential to hold frequent planning sessions, at which progress is evaluated and goals are reviewed, and, if necessary, reformulated. A clear understanding of the group's specific goals and procedures helps students remain oriented and involved.

During the initial planning sessions the teacher behaves as guide and counselor, rather than as director of learning activities. He or she should participate in the cooperative planning, helping students to choose their topic and formulate their suggestions clearly. The teacher should be careful, however, not to undermine the students' awareness of influencing decisions by imposing his or her own suggestions, or dominating the conversation. A teacher making the transition from a traditional class structure to small-group, cooperative learning is advised to keep a written record of the early planning sessions. He or she will want to know who were the main speakers, who said little or nothing, how much the teacher added to the discussion, whether he or she tended to reject suggestions made by certain pupils, and whether he or she culminated the discussion.

The following example is an illustration of supportive guidance on the part of the teacher. The teacher asked the pupils what they would like to study about birds and which questions they wanted answered. At the end of the meeting, the questions to be studied were written on a large placard. When the answer to a question was found, it was recorded on the placard in a space left for that purpose. Note the teacher's role in the following:

Ann: I would like to know about nests.

Teacher: Could you explain what you would like to know about them?

Ann: Are there different kinds, and where do birds build them?

          (The teacher writes the question on the board.)

Jerry: What about the kind of food birds eat?

          (The teacher, with Jerry's permission, writes:
          "What types of food are eaten by birds?")

David: How do they build their nests?

Teacher: Let's compare your question to Ann's. Is there anything similar about them? Let's add your question to that one.

Jackie: Different kinds of birds.

Teacher: Do you mean the different names birds have, or how we can identify different kinds of birds?

          (Jackie says nothing.)

Teacher: Who can help Jackie?

Ronald: How can we recognize different birds?

          (Jackie agrees that the question should be written in the way Ronald phrased it.)

This teacher helped the pupils to formulate their questions well, and suggested additions without inhibiting or suppressing the students. Student-teacher interaction was cooperative. The teacher also accepted different levels of ability and interest.

After recording all the questions, this class organized itself into small groups, each one responsible for investigating one question. This kind of group is generally formed on the basis of the pupils' interest in the topic: each pupil chooses the question he wants to study and joins a group sharing his interest. It will, of course, be necessary to limit the number of pupils investigating any one question, and "empty" groups will have to be filled by a fair means of selection.

The groups then meet to discuss what information they require to answer their question, and to decide who will undertake which research. If, for example, the group investigating nests finds that there are many types, each member might limit his study to one or two types.

The nature of the tasks should not be limited to reading and summarizing. While some students read, others could prepare a display. Younger children might cut out pictures from magazines and prepare charts and explanatory texts to accompany them. The material contributed by all the students could then be used to make a file or a scrapbook, or to construct one large display in which everyone would cooperate. Groups may summarize their findings by presenting a play to the rest of the class, by painting a mural, or even by constructing a learning center for other groups (see Chapter Six for an explanation of learning centers). Naturally, the complexity of the project will depend on the students' age and imaginative abilities. Teachers should encourage inventiveness and active expression of initiative and imagination.

Exercise in cooperative planning. A more structured approach to cooperative planning is found in the following exercise, adapted from Gorman (1969), designed to help students in higher elementary grades and up to acquire the skills necessary for cooperative planning. The exercise seeks to foster group cohesiveness as well as create a cooperative experience for students. At the end of the exercise, which lasts five sessions, students should be better acquainted with each other and should be able to plan together their subject and method of study.

Session one. The teacher begins by offering a broad explanation:

> This is a class in science, in which everyone here had some experience last year. All of you probably have some idea of what we're going to study this year. You also have your own hobbies, interests, experiences, and plans for the future. The project you are about to embark on can help you to know each other better and to express your own ideas about the subject we're studying. This is an opportunity for you to bring your personal interests into your school studies.

The teacher divides the class into pairs of students, each of which meets for five minutes. Then every two pairs form a quartet, and the quartets meet for five minutes. The quartets then form octets, and each octet meets for ten minutes. During a final five-minute session each octet summarizes its discussion.

Each subgroup—of pairs, quartets, and octets—performs two tasks:

1. Each group member tells his or her name, hobbies, and other interests. (This, of course, is only relevant if students are not well acquainted.)

2. Members discuss what they would like to study about the topic in question, both as a group and as individuals. They choose a secretary to record their ideas.

Session two. At the end of the first session the teacher mimeographs the students' notes and distributes copies to all students, who spend the first five minutes of the second session reading them and writing down their comments. Then the class divides up once more into pairs, quartets, and octets. The pairs formed in this session are identical with those in the first session, but the composition of quartets and octets differs so that new acquaintances can be made. Once more everyone performs the same two tasks—introducing themselves and discussing what they want to learn about their topic. Students record their ideas and hand their notes to the teacher.

Session three. Having read over the students' notes from both sessions and organized them into groups of topics, the teacher gives each student a copy of the outline.

The first five minutes of the third session are spent reading the outline and writing comments. The rest of the session is devoted to cooperative planning by teacher and students on how to approach study of their chosen topic. Together they plan which topic will be taught first, which method is the most appropriate, where to look for information, and how to use different sources. Information can come from libraries, books, periodicals, interviews, visits to institutions, films, photographs, and specimens. It is important to help students find out how to seek information within the school as well as outside of it. They may also profit from visiting other schools. Group leadership roles should be delegated to different participants, and their responsibilities, as well as all the subtopics assigned to group members, listed on the blackboard. Before the outset of the work the teacher will probably wish to clarify how the students' work will be integrated and evaluated; whether they will have an exam; whether they should present a written report as individuals or as a group; whether they should prepare a photograph album; or whether they should prepare a file on a particular topic. If all these questions are answered during this session, the students are almost ready to begin their work.

Session four. It is to be hoped that participation in this exercise so far will make students identify as members of a larger group. They have met in different-sized groups and exchanged ideas and opinions. Now they are confronted with the more difficult task of making decisions, particularly about a time schedule for their activities. The fourth session concentrates on formulating a detailed plan of activity for the days, weeks, or months ahead, on the basis of the discussions held during the first three sessions. This session begins with octets, which then combine to form 16-person groups, and finally the class meets as a whole.

Some teachers find that the exchange of ideas in octets and 16's is cumbersome, and choose to conduct the fourth session in quartets only.

The groups are formed and the teacher tells them that their main goal is to decide on a course of action; *what* to do, *who* will do it, and *how long* it will take. While these problems are being discussed, the teacher moves around among the groups and offers suggestions wherever they are needed and are welcome.

The groups formed in this session may remain constant, i.e., the planning groups may continue to execute the actual research. On the other hand, at the end of this session, each student may decide which topic he wishes to investigate, and then students form new groups accordingly.

Session five. During this final meeting of the preparation stage, students summarize all their plans and decisions. Each research group gives the teacher a list of members with their specific roles, and the teacher reviews the list with the group. It is helpful to mimeograph and circulate the list or post it where it is easily available to everyone.

Since the above exercise is their first experience in small-group learning, the pupils' reactions can be a valuable source of improvement. Did they really get to know each other better than in the usual classroom situation? Was it an enjoyable experience? Did they discover anything new about their classmates? Did the experience enhance or detract from their classroom learning? Did they enjoy planning their learning activities?

This exercise can be a first step in developing efficient planning ability, and future planning sessions can be approached without first going through the "getting-acquainted" stage.

Dividing the units into sub-topics. As a result of the fourth and fifth planning sessions, described above, the main unit may be divided in the following manner, in which each small group, represented by the letters A, B, C, etc., undertakes to investigate a different sub-topic. (See Figure 6.)

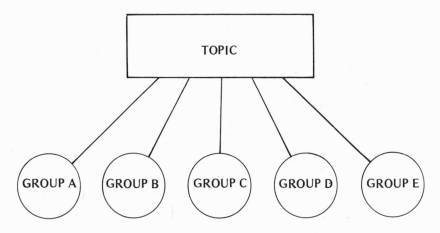

Figure 6. Groups investigating
different sub-topics.

Another way of dividing the larger unit is to have each small group simultaneously investigate *the same* sub-topic. The sub-topic will be changed at regular intervals until all required or relevant aspects of the large unit have been covered. The amount of time devoted to each sub-topic depends on the breadth of the problem and the students' proficiency at working in groups. In the lower grades, or in a class new to group work, the sub-topic may simply be one circumscribed problem, requiring only a day or two of investigation. In the upper grades, or with students who have experienced group study, the sub-topic may be a more complex problem, requiring a week or more of investigation.

At the end of their investigation, groups report their findings to the whole class. Reports may be in many forms, such as a display, a dramatization, a diagram, a map, a scrapbook, or a filmstrip prepared by the small group. It is not always necessary, however, for the small group to share its findings with the whole class, especially if sub-topics are changed at very short intervals (Miel, 1952).

A more complex model for dividing small-group investigation of a major unit is presented in Figure 7 (page 86).

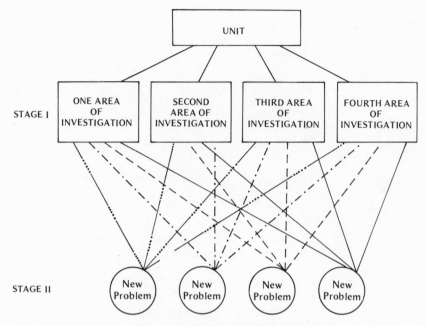

*Figure 7. Two stages in small-group
investigation and problem-solving.*

The investigation is divided into two stages: information-gathering and problem-solving. In the information-gathering stage, each small group explores in depth a different area of the larger unit, the students thus becoming "specialists" in their chosen field. If studying India, for example, one group can study the religions of the country, another its agriculture, another its industry, and so on. Or, the whole class can study India's social structure, with each group investigating a different caste. In the second stage, the teacher presents the students with a new problem, the solution of which demands use of the knowledge acquired in the first stage of investigation. New groups are formed comprised of one or more "specialists" from each of the former groups. Each contributes to the investigation of the problem by informing other group members about his area of specialization and its bearing on the problem. The group's final report or product reflects this pooling of information.

Learning skills. During the project, students will engage in many valuable learning activities:

- learning about and using different sources of infor- mation—books, periodicals, films and filmstrips, maps, trips, experiments, interviews;
- learning to use the school and local library and how to use indices and catalogues; and
- improving research skills, such as distinguishing the relevant from the irrelevant, recording information, preparing outlines of subjects, and assessing the relia- bility of information.

Pupils in the first elementary grades will, of course, need more help than older children in finding information. The teacher might place markers in books containing relevant information, and must be careful to choose books at the appropriate reading level, so that the pupil does not attempt research which is beyond his ability. While the students are working, the teacher can check whether they know how to use an index and understand the vocabulary of the subject. Technical terms which might be encountered frequently are best explained to the entire class before any reading begins. It might be interesting for one group of students to prepare a list of technical terms and definitions to be distributed to the whole class.

The teacher might prepare a checklist of the skills needed for doing research. Students can check their own knowledge against the list and discuss their needs in their groups or with the teacher. The list might include:

- using a table of contents;
- using an index;
- finding words in the dictionary (selecting the appro- priate meaning);
- using encyclopedias; and

- using appendices in reference books.

All of these are critical for independent study at any age level, and it is important for students to master them early. A research project helps students to demonstrate these skills and practice them in a relevant context rather than as a tedious exercise. Group research work can be temporarily interrupted to teach a particular skill when necessary. Students could also be taken out of their various groups and taught collectively a skill they all lack, and then return to their own groups (Burton, 1962).

When each group has completed its project, it may present its findings to the entire class. The reports need not be wholly written or verbal. Students should be encouraged to present their projects in different forms, and not be confined by any set order when organizing their final products. Presentation of findings from scientific experiments (or in social studies or biological or physical sciences), particularly in upper grades and high school, will usually assume more structured forms.

Studying the Environment: An Example

Research into problems affecting the environment can be a valuable experience for students of all ages. A project on some broad issue concerning the environment or a social problem usually has direct bearing on the lives of the student and his family. The relevance of the topic is clear. Such issues include public transportation in the metropolis, freeway construction, the need for new airports, public health problems, housing, saving waterways, the pollution problem in its different manifestations, and inter-ethnic relations.

To examine any of these in depth, students will have to use many techniques, search for information in a variety of sources, and use or acquire skills in many fields: geography, geology, government, chemistry, sociology, statistics, and others. Boundaries between different branches of human knowledge are automatically disregarded in an effort to understand and seek solutions to social problems. The artificiality of the usual academic divisions between one subject and another gives way to interdependence of many kinds of knowledge needed in everyday life. Students can get used to integrating knowledge into a single creation, and experience the excitement of using this knowledge in the struggle to understand and appreciate the world in which they live.

The following project was carried out by an eleventh-grade class and lasted an entire semester, from September to the end of January. Similar projects can be performed at every level, but students must be helped to find information within their level of comprehension.

Transportation problems in our city. *Phase I.* A social studies class in the eleventh grade wanted to be involved in some of the public issues it read and heard about in the news media, notably the construction of a new, controversial cross-town freeway planned by the city and state. To make way for the freeway, many people would be forced to sell their homes. At the same time, the city council was holding hearings about the site of a new municipal airport large enough to accommodate airliners for the next two or three decades. Citizens' groups had been formed to fight the airlines' choice of site because of the ensuing decline of property value in the area. Ecology groups also protested against the chosen site because of its proximity to forest lands; they said that the trees would be affected by constant exposure to exhaust fumes from jet engines. Some students saw it as a clear case of the small man versus the big corporation and city government, whose main interests were financial. Others pointed out that the roads were congested and a new freeway was definitely needed; also that the existing airport was built 15 years ago on a site which was then out of town, but was now close to the town center. People watched big airliners coming in for a landing right above some of the town's most congested streets, so it was not difficult to see that a new airport must be built. Both issues clearly required careful consideration based on knowledge of all the factors involved. Dogmatic opinions could only hold up progress and harm the public. The students themselves realized that they should know more about the problems involved, as the issues would be important for years to come.

The first question was what background information they thought they needed. They made a list of sub-topics for each of the problems. The teacher suggested that the entire class should be involved in working out tentative lists of sub-topics, and should then divide into smaller research groups to investigate the topics. The initial list of topics was compiled by small groups, so that everyone had a chance to speak. (*Buzz groups* are perfect for this purpose.) The 35 students in the class formed nine groups of three and two groups of four. They were allotted 15 minutes to choose a secretary and to make up a list of important issues which they would like to investigate in connection with freeways and airports. Each group dealt with both major topics, one topic on each of two days.

The 15-minute buzz sessions were followed by a panel meeting. The panel consisted of five students (not the secretaries) from different groups. The panel's job was to edit the list of sub-topics written on the blackboard by the group secretaries. This eliminated unnecessary repetition of topics and put all the sub-topics into conceptual categories. The panel was also able to make suggestions of its own. Skillful questioning of panel members by the teacher was necessary to help them formulate the categories into which they would organize the topics. The teacher tried to avoid giving directions to the panel. The entire process, therefore, consisted of the following steps: (1) a general class discussion in which students decided which current issues they wished to study; (2) the formation of buzz groups to compile a list of sub-topics; (3) writing down of the groups' suggestions by their secretaries; (4) editing and organization of the list of sub-topics by the panel; (5) research groups were set up to investigate the topics, and individuals or pairs of students in the groups were responsible for one sub-topic.

The process was completed in four class meetings. The list of topics and sub-topics, after editing by the panel, was as follows:

Freeway Construction

1. *Engineering problems*:
   a.   conceptions of limited-access highways
   b.   construction requirements (measurements, materials, etc.)
   c.   traffic considerations in building (frequency of usage, types of vehicles, congestion expectations, etc.)

2. *Mapping problems*:
   a.   location of road
   b.   connections with other highways
   c.   community traffic needs
   d.   total amount of land presently inhabited

3. *Economic problems*:
   a.   cost of land and property to be purchased
   b.   cost of rehousing families on the site
   c.   cost of construction
   d.   number of bridges, crossovers, etc., needed

4. *Ecological problems*:
   a.   air pollution from exhaust fumes
   b.   effect of noise level on nearby residents
   c.   danger of heavy traffic to children

Airport Construction

1. *Engineering problems*:
   a.   projected size of runways needed for next 20 years
   b.   projected size of passenger terminal (based on estimated population growth and increase in air traffic)
   c.   access to airport, including new roads

2. *Economic problems*:
   a.   loss of property value to nearby inhabitants (as compared with losses at alternative sites)
   b.   cost of land compared with alternative sites
   c.   rise in costs during projected period of construction

3. *Ecological problems*:
    a.   noise pollution and its effect on inhabitants in the vicinity
    b.   air pollution and its effect on surrounding agricultural land and forests
    c.   effect on landscape of roads to the airport

4. *Alternative solutions*:
    a.   other possible sites for the airport and estimate on all factors for each site; cost analysis of alternatives to be weighed against that of main suggestion

5. *Airports and freeways of the future: some guesses*

Students who knew which topic they wanted to study formed the basis of the research groups. Others, less decided, filled out the groups mainly by joining their friends. A remaining few, who were undecided, were assigned to groups by the teacher. Eight groups were formed to cover the eight main sub-divisions of the two topics. The ninth topic (airports and freeways of the future) was left to the end. The teacher thought this could be the subject for a group essay contest after all the research had been completed.

Phase II. Each group elected a chairman to lead the discussion. Before assuming their posts, the chairmen met with the teacher for some hints on the chairman's role (see Chapter Two). The first meeting of the research groups was devoted to answering certain questions:

1.   Who would investigate specific sub-topics?
2.   What were the main sources of information?
3.   Who were the most important people to interview for information? Who were the people likely to know where the relevant information could be found?
4.   How much time would be needed for the investigation?
5.   Were there any other significant sub-topics which the group felt should be studied in order to understand the main issues?

Some groups answered these questions in one 30-minute meeting. Others needed several meetings, as they had to make phone calls and consult with the teacher and other people outside the school. However, almost no new sub-topics were added to the original list. Most everyone felt that the project would last several months. It was therefore important that the groups should meet regularly and keep up to date with reports from members. Without continual support and clarification, individual group members might have strayed from the main point and lost sight of their role in the project.

All the groups were eager to interview relevant people, such as members of the city council and the city planning commission, airline representatives, officers of the various citizens' groups, and professional people who could provide information about the technical aspects of the sub-topics. The prospect of talking to official personalities obviously stirred the students' imagination and added a lot of glamour to the project. School suddenly became part of the "real world," rather than an isolated institution.

The groups prepared questions to ask at the interviews. Each member prepared a list relevant to his own sub-topic, but he had to read his list to, and discuss it with, his own research group. The list was prepared as homework to save group time. The next step was making phone calls to organizations and municipal departments to identify the people to be interviewed.

While students were compiling the list of officials, it suddenly occurred to some that they had never interviewed anyone before. Even with a list of questions they might get flustered and muddled. The teacher then intervened and told them about role playing. It seemed a good idea to practice conducting an interview while they could benefit from fellow-students' comments on their behavior. It was a "safe" way to learn and prevent embarrassment later. The audience clarified many important points of behavior during the post-play session—either the behavior of the student conducting the interview or that of the interviewee (or his secretary, a role which was also included). All students felt they had gained confidence and that the practice would help them conduct a real interview.

Finally, the class had to find names of professional people they would invite to the school to give lectures on related topics and provide them with some technical information. They contacted local branches of professional organizations—engineers, chemists, universities, etc.—and compiled a list of qualified people. Each group composed and typed letters of invitation to these people. They also made phone calls from their homes to make appointments with the officials and organizations they wished to interview. The letter-writing required considerable help from the teacher; although the students had received instructions in writing business letters, few had ever used the knowledge.

At the end of this preparatory stage, which lasted several weeks, the teacher helped the class summarize its plan of investigation. It was decided to approach the issues in several ways:

- obtaining expert advice from professional people not involved in the projects, in order to acquire background information;
- interviewing persons directly involved in the projects or representatives of various organizations who participated in the public hearings; and
- reading published materials to acquire background knowledge.

When the summary was completed and written on the board, the students realized that they had omitted one important source of information: direct study of the sites in question. Someone suggested that the class should make two visits to each site; one at the beginning of their work, so they could visualize the situation clearly, and one toward the end of the project, when they could examine the sites with much more understanding and knowledge.

Parents were asked to help with transportation to interviews. A group of parents formed a carpool and a schedule was set up for two months, during which time all the interviews would take place. Many of the interviews were scheduled during school hours. The transportation was particularly helpful as students decided to take tape recorders with them—an easier way of keeping a record than taking notes.

Each group interviewed from three to six persons during the two allotted months, and the students usually interviewed in pairs. During the same period six guest lecturers came to the class—three for each of the two major topics. The class read and discussed new information, which the teacher located. The reading matter came primarily from the local university library, as little of relevance could be found in either the school or the public library. In order to help students read this material, the teacher found he had occasionally to teach reading and writing skills, such as suggestions for keeping a card catalogue of information, how to compile a bibliography, and how to use bibliographies. He also made arrangements with parents about transportation to and supervision in the university libraries, and transportation of the entire class for the site visits.

Phase III. The final phase of the project took place after the winter vacation. Each research group reread, evaluated, and synthesized into a single report all the information it had gathered. This meant that every student prepared a complete report on the information he had acquired, and this report was then reviewed by the group (copies were given to all the group members). Two or three meetings were devoted to each report, and the writing and discussion of the reports took over three weeks. The project neared completion toward the end of January, close to the end of the semester. A representative of each group presented a 20-minute summary of his group's findings to the entire class. It was decided that a small panel of students should again edit the reports and prepare a single class report based on the groups' findings.

This process required another two weeks. Any questions arising from the reports were addressed to the appropriate group. Finally, the class report was sent to the school board, where it was typed. A copy was sent to the mayor, the city council, the city planning commission, the people who were interviewed, and each of the students who participated in the project.

The class was invited to the mayor's office and received a special citation for its remarkable efforts. A meeting of all the parents was held and they heard the final report presented by several class representatives.

The teacher suggested that with their extensive knowledge of the problems involved in these issues, the students were in an excellent position to write a simulation game called "A New Airport," which was planned for the next semester.

Chapter Five

Group Discussion

Small-group learning requires more than just a random exchange of ideas among group members; extensive discussions of specific topics are often necessary, and the nature of each topic must be defined and understood by all the students involved in studying it. All the group members must be able to gather relevant information from various sources. Therefore, a problem requiring a simple "yes" or "no" answer is inappropriate for group study, as is one which can easily be solved by one person. Suitable tasks are those which stimulate intellectual effort and encourage individual contributions from all members.

The main means of group communication is discussion, which takes place at every stage of the study. Through it the group clarifies and evaluates its problems. The purpose of group discussion can be to outline the research topic, decide upon modes of behavior, plan a specific activity, define learning procedures, or present research findings. At the initial stage of the project, when the class subdivides into small groups, the groups will decide, through discussion, how to set about their chosen task. Later on, discussions can be held to judge the effectiveness of their methods, evaluate the work already completed, and, if necessary, decide upon new research projects based on this work. In other words, such discussions focus attention constantly on the task, clarify problems, and enable the groups to move steadily toward their goal.

A cooperative spirit among students sharing a common purpose should ensure a worthwhile discussion. This does not mean that the students must always agree: discussion allows for the expression of differing, even contradictory, opinions, but it should not be competitive. Group members will undoubtedly wish to influence each other, but they should approach the discussion as equals and grant others the right to speak. They should acknowledge and react to others' comments and try to arrive at decisions based on all the contributions, thereby strengthening the feeling of cooperation in the group. Even those who oppose the decisions will accept them more readily if their own views have also been given a fair hearing.

A well-defined plan will help the discussion achieve its goal and allow free expression of ideas. Students meeting as a discussion group for the first time will be unsure of what is expected of them or how to proceed. The group chairman—who is usually one of the students, but may occasionally be the teacher—opens the discussion by stating its aim, rules of procedure, and time limits. (The many aspects of the chairman's task are discussed later in this chapter.) In short, productive discussion depends on four basic skills: (1) clear planning, (2) effective discussion leadership, (3) total and constructive participation, and (4) the ability to evaluate the discussion and its outcome.

Clear Planning

Clarifying the topic. The aim of discussion is usually to clarify a specific problem. The first step, therefore, is to make sure that all the participants understand the subject under discussion. Here are some basic principles for conducting discussions.

Formulating the topic. The way in which the problem is presented has considerable influence on the discussion. It is better to phrase it as a question than as a general statement: a question defines and limits the scope of discussion more than a statement. For example, asking "How can we reduce the use of school supplies?" presents the problem more effectively than merely stating "The discussion will deal with the problem of excessive use of school supplies." If a group is to discuss as complex an issue as "The problem of delinquency," each member might concentrate on a different aspect: the increase in delinquency, ways of preventing it, family influence, delinquency in urban as opposed to rural areas, and so on. The students will soon realize that they are, in fact, talking about many subjects and that a productive discussion is unlikely to develop. Each of these topics could be the subject of separate discussions in a series devoted to delinquency in general. An attempt to deal with all the topics in a single discussion would result in frustration and dissatisfaction. A question, on the other hand, can point the discussion in a specific direction and thereby increase its effectiveness; limited scope prevents deviation from the main issue (Gulley, 1968).

When presenting a problem, care should be taken not to include the solution in the wording. Compare, for example, the two following questions: "How can we get rid of the inefficient or irresponsible librarian without interrupting library service?" and "What can we do to improve the efficiency of our library?" In the first, a solution is suggested even before discussion has begun, which can only have a negative effect on the ensuing discussion. Students may feel restricted and reluctant to put forward suggestions which they might feel are irrelevant to the one already presented. It may even be found, on closer investigation, that the librarian is not at fault at all (Brilhart, 1967).

The aim of discussion is to bring to light all factors relevant to the topic, how much the participants know about it, and what their opinions are. It should focus on one issue so that this can be explored thoroughly and many possible solutions found. The group should not, however, be compelled to find an answer, even to an issue presented as a question. It is also valuable to discuss a problem simply to acquire more information about it, without necessarily searching for solutions.

It is a good idea for group members to acquire knowledge of a topic independently, by whatever means, before the discussion, so that they all share some common experience. The discussion then gives them a chance to exchange ideas, reactions, and opinions. Prior to the discussion the chairman, alone or together with other group members, should prepare a list of questions to help direct the discussion. The group should decide which questions to tackle at a particular session, and which to postpone. The questions could be listed on a board hung in a prominent place in the classroom; it might be easier and clearer to group them according to related ideas or time sequences.

If it is found that the students are not well enough informed, they can delay the discussion and form research groups. Once they have found the necessary information, they can return to the discussion better equipped to find a solution.

To sum up, the following points should be used as a guide for clarifying the topic to be discussed:

1. What is the problem? Is it clear to everyone?
2. What are the limits of the discussion? How much time is available? What is the scope of the problem? Should it be broken down into sub-topics? Does any particular procedure need to be planned as a product of the discussion? Is the group capable of putting its decision into action?
3. What information do the participants have? What sources do they have access to? How can further information be obtained?

Arriving at a solution. The way in which a discussion is concluded depends, of course, on the type of discussion. If it is planning the subjects to be investigated, then the solution reached should specify the topic as well as the way it is to be approached by the group. If, however, the subject of discussion is, say, the qualities of a work of art, then its aim is education and gratification, and the group members do not need to reach a practical decision.

In an action-group (one which is to reach a practical decision), additional questions should be asked. Can the decision reached be put into effect? Are there other possible solutions? By what criteria are the solutions evaluated? After these points have been clarified, the group formulates a final statement of the solution and distributes tasks to all members.

The group has still to decide how to evaluate its results—a question which is usually asked after the discussion. If, however, it is considered to be of particular importance, it can be dealt with at the beginning. Criteria for judging the results can be set up early in the discussion, so that advantages and disadvantages of particular suggestions can be weighed during the discussion itself.

The chairman will not always be able to prevent deviation from the topic. The discussion should be flexible and participants should not be obliged to keep to a strict program, which might only make the discussion an unpleasant experience for all. Nevertheless, preparing an outline before or at the beginning of the discussion can help the chairman fulfill his role effectively, help group members cope with the major issues, and minimize digressions.

Using an outline as a guide does not necessarily guarantee a systematic and logical discussion. Some experts maintain that group discussion should follow John Dewey's stages of logical thinking, namely:

(1) defining the problem;

(2) analyzing the problem;

(3) suggesting solutions;

(4) examining the advantages and disadvantages of the proposed solution; and

(5) checking the validity of the solution.

In practice, however, discussions do not always develop logically. Participants wander away from the subject, get involved in discussions of side issues, and introduce ideas which are only vaguely related to the main topic. But despite the digressions, discussion groups do reach conclusions and decisions. An emotional approach usually dominates the early stages, when the participants clarify their thinking and offer initial suggestions. Later, the discussion becomes more rational, more centered on the main issues, more critical of the solutions offered (Bormann, 1969). The progress of discussion is, in fact, wave-like, each wave encompassing new ideas, agreements, disagreements, outlooks, and facts. The discussion highlights points on which group members already agree to some extent; very controversial points are ultimately rejected. Questions are dealt with only superficially in the early "waves" of discussion; more thorough investigation comes later, when students begin to feel they are getting to the heart of the matter (Scheidel and Crowell, 1964).

A discussion outline can be effective not only in advanced classes, but also in the lower elementary grades, where pupils can practice stating their goals. With younger students it is advisable to prepare an outline for each subtopic and to discuss each one separately. The information needed for the discussion can be acquired from direct observation, not just from reading. Such objects as seeds, rocks, animals, or even events can all be examined before discussion.

A third-grade class prepared a Safety-First campaign for the whole school. The teacher wrote on the board an outline for the discussion of one sub-topic on the issue of safety in the school. The children discussed several accidents which had occurred in school, and at the end of the discussion a short summary of the group's decisions was recorded on a placard hung on the wall. The conclusions reached led to a formulation of the problem which served as a guide for the entire campaign. A second discussion produced a list of steps in the campaign. The following summary presents the group's goals.

Topic: "How to improve safety in our school."
1.   We shall conduct a discussion to establish the safety rules which should be observed in school.

2. We shall prepare placards with drawings illustrating safety rules.
3. Committees from this class will explain the rules to all the classes in the school.
4. We shall consider, in a later discussion, comments and suggestions made to our committees by other students and consequently shall improve the safety rules.

This summary serves three functions: it presents the subject to the class clearly; it reminds the class what is to be done after the discussion; and it defines the subject of a further discussion.

Preparing for discussion. Careful planning by the students will raise the level of a discussion. Investigation prior to discussion produces valuable information and makes the students better qualified to evaluate others' contributions to the discussion (Brilhart, 1967).

One way of ensuring adequate preparation is to distribute well-defined responsibilities to group members (see Chapter Three). A ninth-grade class discussed the question: "Was the Greek city-state based on democratic principles?" Students consulted relevant sources and, singly and in pairs, assumed responsibility for presenting different aspects.

This type of learning discussion makes it possible to deal in depth with ideas expressed by group members or by outside experts invited to the school to participate in the discussion. It is also possible to examine a topic from a number of different perspectives. If, before the discussion, students are aware of the differing viewpoints to their topic—particularly if the topic is controversial—they will be more tolerant of other people's views. The discussion will then be an opportunity for examining ideas, not a tug-of-war between the uninformed.

Following are suggestions for students of steps in preparing the background information for a discussion (Brilhart, 1967):

1. Prepare a list of all that is known about the subject at present. The following suggestions will help in the preparation of the list:

A. Try to get a general view of the entire problem. To what is it related? What are the factors influencing it and how can it influence other events? For example, a discussion on "Accepting a new student into the class" should consider the newcomer's place of origin, the schools he attended, what subjects are new for him in this school, how much he knows about the subjects the class is studying now, and which students in the class are most able to help him adjust socially to his new environment.

B. Prepare a list of everything you know about the subject: what you have read, seen, and heard; any relevant practical experience; your own ideas on the subject. Write down, freely and without critical reservations, anything which comes to mind about the subject.

C. Organize all your information according to an outline.

D. Go over the outline and look for information still missing. What aspects of the problem are still unclear? Do any of the hypotheses still require clarification or further information?

2. Find missing information in the appropriate sources and record the important facts. One convenient way of keeping notes is on small file cards; at the top of each card should be a heading as in a bibliography, and a summary of the information will fill the rest of the card, as shown here:

> *Topic:*   "The idea of justice in ancient Greece."
> *Source:* Jaeger, Werner—*Paideia: The Ideals of Greek Culture.*
>   Vol. I. Oxford University Press, New York, 1945.
>   Chapter 6 (p. 99ff): The City-State and Its Ideal of
>   Justice.
> p. 104   "Early Greece strove, above everything else, for equal
>   justice. . . ."

3. Evaluate the information gathered and your hypotheses. Some of the hypotheses first suggested may no longer be valid because of contradictory evidence uncovered later. Review the information carefully and ask yourself some of the following questions: Are your sources reliable? Are they unbiased? Is information from one source contradicted by information from

another? If you are relying on the opinion of one person, is he acknowledged to be an expert in the subject?

Preparing the background to a discussion in this way is appropriate for students in upper elementary grades, high school, and university. With some changes, it can also be accomplished by lower elementary school classes, who could prepare for a discussion by reading, seeing a film or filmstrip, or hearing a short lecture. Perhaps the teacher will want to summarize the information gathered during the preparation stage and, together with the students, record the summary as an outline. Preparing for a discussion is a basic learning skill which can be acquired by students in the lower grades and utilized independently in later years.

Effective Discussion Leadership

Leading a discussion. Leadership develops during the discussion. Anyone who influences other participants contributes to the progress of the discussion and plays a role in leading the group. His influence comes from his clear concept of the group's goals, and his ability to keep the group focused on the central issue and to resolve misunderstandings. Good leadership moves the group toward its goals and limits disruptive behavior, though this does not mean that an authoritarian approach is necessary. There can be several leaders representing various aspects of the leadership role; it is rare to find all the required leadership skills in one person. One group member may clarify the problem, another supply additional information, another ask penetrating questions, and another be capable of decreasing tension in the group.

However, even when these skills are dispersed among members, it is important to choose a chairman, to have someone responsible for seeing that all the leadership roles are carried out, or, if necessary, to perform them himself. There must be a distinction between the selected chairman and a participant whose leadership status develops during the discussion. In a group which meets frequently, the function of the chairman should be to open the discussion, and thereafter he should participate on the same level as the other members, sharing leadership roles with them. Some of the skills required of a discussion leader were presented in Chapter Two. They fall into two categories: administrative, concentrating on achieving the group goal, and social, concentrating on human relations in the group and maintaining a free flow of communication. A chairman needs to direct activities, evaluate suggestions, and promote cooperation among group members (Bormann, 1969; Brilhart, 1967; Gulley, 1968; Miel, 1952).

Directing activities.

A. Opening the discussion: The chairman presents the topic, informs the group of any time limits, and distributes written material available, including summaries of previous discussions. Alternatively, he could write this information on the blackboard. It is often helpful to hand out copies of the outline he prepared as a discussion guide, but this too can be written on the board. In advanced classes the outline might be quite complex, and other students might suggest alterations, so a secretary will have to be chosen to record all comments.

B. Focusing the discussion on the topic: In order to ensure that the discussion is restricted to the topic, the chairman will occasionally have to restate the topic and remind everyone of the goal. A tactful way to do this would be to ask: "How will that suggestion help us reach our goal?" or say "I'm afraid your remarks do not answer the question. Maybe you can say it in some other way?" or "The subject you are talking about will be discussed after we have talked more about the question before us now." Naturally, students must learn to say these things in a friendly way and avoid arousing hostility or offending people.

In the lower elementary grades the teacher most often serves as chairman. He or she must be tolerant of comments having no direct bearing on the subject. Students of that age have not yet acquired discussion skills and the teacher should not be over-optimistic. It is important to increase young students' self-confidence and awareness of their right to take an active part in discussions; thus, criticism of every digression from the topic is not desirable. The teacher should follow a flexible system, leading the discussion in such a way that students will focus on the topic to a reasonable extent, without damaging anyone's self-esteem (Miel, 1952).

If someone suggests a solution too early in the discussion, he can be asked to repeat it later, when the group has considered all the factors. If there is a tendency to repeat previous suggestions and no new ideas are produced, then perhaps the group is ready to move on to a new topic. If the group agrees that this is the case, then all current information should be summarized and the next issue presented. In this way, transition from one topic to the next will be quite clear. It is important to refer to the outline from time to time to check that all important points are being included in the discussion. At the end of the discussion, a clear summary should be made, covering all the main decisions resulting from the discussion, clarifying the division of responsibilities among group members, and stating whether additional discussions will be needed. Thanking everyone, including the chairman, adds a pleasant note to the proceedings.

C. Encouraging maximum participation by all students: No one should be under any obligation to speak or be prevented from expressing himself. The chairman should watch for signs that someone would like to talk. If a usually reticent student appears to have something to say, the chairman could ask him directly if he would like to speak, leaving him free to reply "not now" with little embarrassment. This is a better approach than the blunt question: "What do you think?"

Encouraging participation is one of the chairman's main roles. Teachers serving as chairmen will have to control their criticism of incorrect statements; helping students to overcome their anxiety about saying something "wrong" is not easy, and they may feel that silence is safer—it is always preferable to criticism. An atmosphere of acceptance should therefore be cultivated, one in which students feel that their contributions are valuable and taken seriously. An understanding teacher would say: "Yes, we'll have to consider that suggestion," or "It's good that you brought up that point," rather than dismissing suggestions with: "We can't discuss that subject," "That's wrong," or "You spoke out of turn"—comments which would silence quite a few students and generally dampen motivation (Gulley, 1968).

If the chosen topic is unclear or unrelated to the students' personal experience, discussion will be difficult. The teacher must be certain that the topic and discussion goals are clear to all participants. Even if the goal is planning a party, those who do not know party games, or cannot act, sing, or read aloud, might be reluctant to take part. Illustrating the ideas under discussion can encourage active participation. One easily available aid is the blackboard, on which both the outline of the discussion and the students' contributions can be written. The students can also be asked to provide drawings, tables, or any other visual aid. These media often clarify at a glance what much talk fails to explain (Miel, 1952).

There are invariably one or two group members who try to monopolize the discussion, and the chairman must try to restrain them tactfully and, as far as possible, ensure equal participation by all students. The chairman can stop a particularly verbose member at the end of a sentence with "What do the others think about that suggestion?" He can also ask everyone at the beginning of the discussion to try to make one contribution when his turn comes. When the chairman asks a question, he should avoid looking at the "talkers" and concentrate on the "non-talkers." Finally, a note should be kept of the number of contributions by each individual, including the teacher and chairman. The group can then see in retrospect if the discussion was dominated by anyone in particular, and if so by whom. It can not be expected that all students will speak with equal frequency—this is a rare occurrence indeed—but a situation in which the talk is really monopolized by certain students requires correction.

In addition to fostering a spirit of mutual support, the teacher can promote productive discussion by the use of games devised for this purpose. The rules of one such game are that each participant must make at least one contribution without prompting from other students. The more contributions and the sooner they are made, the more points the group will get. This creates pressure on the hesitant group members, and at the same time will make the more outspoken students encourage them. The game procedure is as follows: The class divides into two groups sitting in circles, with the teacher sitting at the side. The teacher presents a problem within the students' own experience, such as "What is the best TV program in this country?" or "In what ways can we improve our school?" It is preferable for students to talk in random order, rather than according to their seating plan. The group that wins is the one which arrives at an agreement in the least time. Afterwards the groups evaluate their performance. How did they decide on the order in which members would talk? Who was responsible for keeping order? How were reticent students encouraged to speak out? If the game does not stimulate enough participation the first time, it can be repeated with a slight change in the rules. This time two points will be awarded for the first contribution and one point for each contribution thereafter. At the end of the allotted time (about ten minutes) the group must summarize its activities. The winner is the group with the most points (Stanford and Stanford, 1969).

Evaluating contributions. In a suitably positive atmosphere, evaluation of contributions to the discussion can be a valuable experience for students. Evaluation should not mean criticism, but should attempt to show the relevance of students' remarks and clarify ambiguous statements. It should be clear that it is the *contribution* which is being evaluated and not the student himself.

A group of kindergarten children choosing names for two fish kept in the class suggested many alternatives, including their own names or those of their friends. Remarking on this, the teacher said "We have only two fish, but many children, and it would be hard to decide which of your names to choose. Let's look closely at the fish and see if we can find a name that fits them. How do they look? What do they do?" The children noted that the fish had spots, that one had larger scales than the other, etc., so that the names "Dotty" and "Scaly" were decided upon. Thus, the teacher explained to the children in simple terms the shortcomings of their approach, without direct criticism of the children, and suggested an alternative. No one was embarrassed, no one was made to feel inadequate, and no suggestions were impatiently rejected (Miel, 1952).

Older children can and should evaluate their own contributions, if necessary with guiding questions from the teacher, such as:

- How do your remarks relate to the topic?
- What is the similarity between your comment and the situation we are discussing?
- What is the source of your information?
- Do experts in this field share that opinion?
- Is there information which contradicts or modifies yours?

The chairman should encourage everyone to examine his suggestions against the background of all the knowledge the group has. Questions such as these should be asked:

- Is there any proof that this solution is appropriate or inappropriate?
- Is this solution supported by facts?
- Does the solution get to the heart of the matter or is it superficial?
- Can we check the effectiveness of the solution before making a final decision?

Clarifying communications. In the early stages of group work, students often fail to pay attention when others speak. The following games enable teachers to encourage attentive listening.

A game for developing equal distribution of speaking privileges in a group. Students are seated in a circle. The teacher stands outside the circle and explains the game as follows: Today we are going to play a game that will help improve our discussion skills. I am holding a set of clues that will help you solve a murder mystery. If you put all the clues together, you will be able to solve the mystery. You must find the *murderer,* the *weapon,* the *time* of the murder, the *place* of the murder, and the *motive.* When you think you know the answers and the group agrees on the solution, let me know. Organize yourselves in any way you feel is appropriate. You may not pass your clues around or show them to anyone else. Please do not leave your seats to walk around. Share all your ideas and clues *verbally.*

If there are more than 22 students, the teacher may make up extra clues or several students may share clues. Some students should serve as observers and timekeepers. The observers can make suggestions about how the group could better organize itself and work faster.

Following are the clues, which should be typed in such a way that they can be cut out and put on separate cards:

- When he was discovered dead, Mr. Thompson had a bullet hole in his calf and a knife wound in his back.
- Mr. Barton shot at an intruder in his apartment building at midnight.
- Mr. Thompson had virtually wiped out Mr. Barton's business by stealing his customers.
- The elevator operator reported to the police that he saw Mr. Thompson at 12:15 a.m.
- The bullet taken from Mr. Thompson's calf matched the gun owned by Mr. Barton.
- Only one bullet had been fired from Mr. Barton's gun.
- The elevator man said that Mr. Thompson did not seem too badly hurt.
- A knife found in the parking garage had been wiped clean of fingerprints.

- Mrs. Scott had been waiting in the lobby for her husband to get off work.
- The elevator man went off duty at 12:30 a.m.
- Mr. Thompson's body was found in the park.
- Mr. Thompson's body was found at 1:20 a.m.
- Mr. Thompson had been dead for about an hour when his body was found, according to the medical examiner.
- Mrs. Scott did not see Mr. Thompson leave through the lobby while she was waiting.
- Bloodstains corresponding to Mr. Thompson's blood type were found in the basement parking area.
- Police were unable to locate Mr. Barton after the murder.
- Mr. Thompson's blood type was found on the carpet outside Mr. Barton's apartment.
- There were bloodstains in the elevator.
- Mrs. Scott had been a good friend of Mr. Thompson and had often visited his apartment.
- Mrs. Scott's husband had been jealous of the friendship.
- Mrs. Scott's husband did not appear in the lobby at 12:30 a.m., the end of his normal working hours. She had to return home alone and he arrived later.
- At 12:45 a.m. Mrs. Scott could not find her husband or the family car in the basement parking lot of the apartment building where he worked.

ANSWER: After receiving a superficial gunshot wound from Mr. Barton, Mr. Thompson stepped on the elevator and was killed by Mr. Scott, the elevator man, with a knife at 12:30 a.m., because Mr. Scott was jealous.

The main question a group should keep in mind when evaluating this exercise is: how did it succeed in solving the mystery? In order to answer this, students should then ask themselves specific questions: Did the group need a chairman? How much time was spent on organization? Why was it inefficient for everyone to try to talk at once? Once they have found an answer to all these questions, they will understand how they communicate with each other and will be able to apply the same techniques to future discussions.

The group should also talk about the importance of encouraging each student to make a contribution and of taking other people's ideas into account. If the game was not successful, it should be repeated with a new set of clues. The teacher must be sure that each clue contributes an important piece of information for solving the crime. Another evaluation session should follow the second game (Johnson and Johnson, 1975; Stanford and Stanford, 1969).

A game to encourage listening. Many students think that discussions are arguments or debates, but they must learn that a productive discussion is based on cooperation. A suitable topic is one which arouses people to take a position, such as: "Should mercy killing be legalized?" or "Is capitalism preferable to socialism?" One student is asked to express his opinion, and another to react to this opinion. The second speaker should summarize the first one's comments to show that he understood them, and then explain why and to what extent he agrees with them. He should mention only the points of agreement and ignore any disagreement. When he has completed his comments, he then becomes the speaker and only then may he state his reservations about the first speaker's ideas. When he has finished speaking, a third student is asked to react to his comments, and so on, until each member has both spoken and expressed his reactions (Stanford and Stanford, 1969).

Emotion and logic in discussion. For the sake of clear communication during a discussion, emotional language and the expression of prejudices are best avoided (Brilhart, 1967; Gulley, 1968). That does not mean that participants must agree or accept the majority opinion. It is the chairman's responsibility to reduce tensions and keep the discussion on as rational a level as possible. He should occasionally repeat the common group goal and should use the word "we" to emphasize cohesiveness. All comments should be objective and no remarks should be directed at individuals. Tension can be eased with humor, which adds spontaneity and pleasure to the group's work. Even if contradictory solutions to a problem are suggested, the group should try to agree on a plan of action. A solution acceptable to all can be arrived at through compromise.

Total and Constructive Participation

The stand taken by the speakers will be determined by their own opinions, but they must be willing to compromise for the sake of the group goal. This will afford them both personal gratification and a feeling of involvement in the collective effort.

The following guidelines might be helpful for developing effective group participation. The students should approach the discussion with the greatest possible objectivity; that is, a willingness to take into consideration all the points of view presented. Every suggested solution to the problem should be closely examined, regardless of whether it is in agreement with the individual's own viewpoint—but it need not be accepted passively. The right attitude is of paramount importance, and the students must be flexible and bear the group goal in mind constantly.

All participants must be aware of their right to express themselves, although, of course, some will make more valuable contributions than others. Those who are interested in having their ideas adopted by the group will make sure they are well informed and have prepared their statements for the discussion. An outline, as noted previously, can help speakers present their ideas systematically.

Participation skills. Listeners' interest is aroused not only by ideas themselves but by the way in which they are presented. There are six points worth bearing in mind when addressing a group (Brilhart, 1967; Gulley, 1968):

1. A speaker should talk neither too loudly nor too softly. An inaudible voice creates the impression that the speaker is not interested in the group. Shouting repels listeners, generates tension, and appears overemotional and irrational.
2. The speaker should address himself to the group as a whole and not to a few individuals. Even when answering a specific question, he should look at everyone. If he concentrates on one person, the impact of his words is lessened.

3. Comments should be presented in an orderly way: the speaker should first refer back to the previous speaker's remarks, then present his own ideas (with sources of information), then explain the relevance of these ideas to the group issue.

4. The speaker should raise only a few points at a time. A presentation loaded with too many issues confuses and imposes too great a burden on listeners.

5. Each single contribution should be short. Following the kind of outline suggested here helps speakers limit their remarks. Long speeches are boring and deprive other speakers of time.

6. Language must be clear and straightforward. It is important for all members to listen carefully, so that time is not wasted on needless repetition, and everything is clearly understood. Close attention requires effort, but this will develop with experience, and the development process is greatly aided by the group's own evaluation of its activities.

Evaluation of Discussion and Outcome

Evaluation should measure the group's activities without judgment. Its aim is not to give grades or personal recommendations, but to improve communication and awareness of appropriate group behavior. The main question is whether the students achieved their goal, and the answers must come from the students, not the teacher.

Evaluation in lower grades. In the early elementary grades, evaluation should take place frequently (Flanders, 1954). After each stage in their work, pupils should ask whether they are progressing toward their goal and whether their procedures are the right ones. In a discussion which is one of a series, a few minutes at the end should be devoted to such questions as "How can we improve cooperation in the group?" and "How can we make tomorrow's work more efficient then today's?" These questions encourage the children to keep the collective purpose in mind and to evaluate contributions. They also reduce individual criticism by looking forward to improved group functioning rather than backward to one member's inefficiency.

The criteria of evaluation should be decided upon before the discussion so that group members know what is expected of them. They should ask themselves how reliable was the information presented, how closely related each contribution was to the group goal, how efficient was the general discussion, how cohesive was the group, to what extent members participated, and whether the group leadership was satisfactory. Non-verbal contributions—drawings, summaries, graphs, displays—should also be evaluated. Once students have learned to evaluate and make decisions about group activities, they will know how to cooperate and behave responsibly and will feel they have an active part in formulating their studies.

Evaluation in higher grades. In upper elementary and higher grades, evaluation can rely more directly on questionnaires and other written materials. Groups should formulate their own questionnaires appropriate to their purpose, and evaluation should be a routine part of the procedure.

If, during the discussion, the group feels that its progress is unsatisfactory, then the current work should be interrupted and the problems investigated. If specific skills are found to be lacking, the students can decide how to acquire them in order to accelerate the group's progress.

Evaluation concentrates on four aspects of group activity:
(1) the character of the group, including personal relations and cohesiveness;
(2) its productivity and what it produces;
(3) individual participation; and
(4) leadership.

Each group should prepare an evaluation questionnaire of its own, but the following samples can serve as a guide. In general, a positive answer indicates progress and a negative one some group inadequacy (Benne, Bradford, and Lippitt, 1951).

I. *Evaluation of group functioning.*

1. Did all members participate in the discussion?
2. Did all participants understand the importance of the problem?
3. Was the purpose of the discussion to decide upon a course of action?
4. Did the group recognize differences of opinion and try to reconcile them?
5. Did the group recognize the need to obtain information? Did members know where to find information?
6. Does the group know how to utilize various sources of information—including knowledgeable people—as a basis for an informed discussion?
7. Is the group too dependent on its leaders?
8. Does an atmosphere of friendly cooperation prevail in the group, particularly when contradictory ideas are expressed?
9. Does the group resist domination by any one person?
10. Is the group realistically capable of discussing the subject it chose?

II. *Extent of free expression.*

1. Is there a relaxed or rigid atmosphere?
2. Does everyone make a contribution?
3. Do group members know how to encourage each other?
4. Do group members feel the topic is important and worthy of discussion?

III. *Extent of acceptance in the group.*

1. Are members friendly to each other?
2. Do they enjoy exchanging ideas?
3. Does their behavior indicate respect for each other?

IV. *Extent of group cohesiveness.*
   1.   Do group members anticipate reactions from one another?
   2.   Do they try to persuade opponents to agree with their point of view?
   3.   Is the atmosphere competitive or cooperative?
   4.   Do members concentrate on the group goal or on themselves?

V. *Efficiency of group communication.*
   1.   Are most of the contributions addressed to the group as a unit or to individuals?
   2.   Do participants listen to each other?
   3.   Do speakers refer to comments made by others?

Before answering a questionnaire, members should decide which areas of group functioning need evaluation, and also how to interpret the results. In other words, before beginning their evaluation, each member must understand what the results will mean for the group.

Evaluating group productivity. A group planning a course of action will wish to evaluate its decisions. The best time for this is after the decisions have been carried out, so that the results can be seen and evaluated. There are, however, other ways in which the discussion can be evaluated so that students can see how it influences decision-making. Students can ask what the advantages of their decisions are, to what extent participants are satisfied with them, and to what extent they are committed to carrying them out.

Another way to assess the effectiveness of the group is to conduct observations *during* the discussion. The observer may be a member of the group, a member of another group, or the teacher. He judges the discussion according to criteria agreed upon before the discussion, and, at the end, reports his findings to the group. Since he does not participate in the discussion, his judgment is likely to be objective. He could use questions such as these as a basis:

1. How much time was spent discussing irrelevant matters?
2. How much digression was there from the topic?
3. To what extent did group members help the chairman lead the discussion?
4. Was the discussion adequate or superficial?
5. Were several alternative solutions suggested?
6. Was every possible solution explored?
7. How much time was devoted to each alternative?
8. How many group members contributed to the discussion?

Since the observer's findings will doubtlessly reflect his personal impression of the discussion, it is best for the group to agree in advance on the questions he must answer and be sure that they are fully clarified to all concerned, including the observer.

The role of the observer. A participant in a discussion is not free enough to judge developments objectively. The role can be better performed by an outsider. Observation is a highly instructive experience, and every student should have the opportunity to try it. Afterwards, students' participation in the discussion will probably be more effective.

When students are engrossed in talking, they often forget basic procedures established before the discussion. The observer may remind them of these procedures without criticizing the group. He may also intervene if the group reaches an impasse, or if the chairman fails to clarify some point. He could make a neutral remark, such as "perhaps the group doesn't realize that three different subjects have been introduced during the past five minutes" or, if the group has spent too long on one subject, "maybe we are ready to suggest possible solutions" (Brilhart, 1967).

It is wise to find out participants' own reactions to their discussion. Each group member can answer a few questions immediately after the discussion and the answers are tallied. The group can then hold a short meeting to examine its reactions and thereby improve its discussion technique. Suitable questions would be (Brilhart, 1967):

1.   Were you satisfied with the discussion?

Very   in general   not at all

2.   How would you evaluate the chairman's behavior during the discussion?

Authoritarian   democratic   weak

3.   Did you want to speak but fail to get the opportunity?

No   sometimes   often

Evaluating individuals and the chairman. There is no doubt that the attitude and skill of each group member considerably influence the character of the discussion. The teacher will naturally wish to help students improve their skills, but he or she must be careful not to pay too much attention to individuals at the expense of the group, which is, after all, the critical unit here. It is important for members to be aware that they constitute a cohesive group and not simply a *collection* of independent individuals. If an individual student does not become integrated into the group, the teacher can speak to him in private, but no person should be singled out as a scapegoat. The group as a unit must bear responsibility for its own activities.

The chairman's position, however, is slightly different. Since he is fulfilling a role and not being "himself," the role can be separated from the person. As many students will be chairman at some time, it is important that the role should be thoroughly clarified. The observer can work from a prepared questionnaire such as this (Gulley, 1968):

Questionnaire for Evaluating the Chairman

1.   Does he treat participants with respect? Is he sensitive to them?
2.   Does he listen to speakers and consider their views and comments?
3.   Does he provide an adequate explanation of the problem being discussed?
4.   Does he know how to redirect the discussion when it digresses?

5. Does he know how to help the group achieve its goal?
6. Does he keep order and prevent disruption of the discussion?
7. Does he encourage cooperation among members?
8. Does he resolve disagreements and emphasize points of agreement?
9. Does he know how to end the discussion?

Observation-feedback exercise. Conducting effective discussions requires practice. An interesting way for groups to improve their discussion skills is to have student observers view a discussion, report their findings to the group, and then have the group conduct a new discussion in light of the observers' comments. One way to carry out this "observation-feedback" exercise is with the "fishbowl" technique, as follows: A small group of discussants sit in the innermost of three circles (or half-circles). The second circle of chairs is occupied by several observers. Members of the class sit in the outermost circle. Or, the teacher may wish to hold several fishbowl-discussions simultaneously, so that all students can participate as discussants or observers. In that case, there would be no third circle of spectators.

The inner group will conduct a short discussion (perhaps 10 minutes for younger, 20 minutes for older students) while observers analyze the group process. This analysis can be aided by the use of a questionnaire with rating scales or by an observation schedule. These schedules help observers record who says or does what and with what frequency particular acts are performed (Napier and Gershenfeld, 1973; Schmuck and Runkel, 1972; Schmuck and Schmuck, 1974). Following are some examples:

Questionnaires and rating scales. Observers could use existing questionnaires, such as those suggested in this chapter, or construct their own with some guidance from the teacher (Schmuck and Runkel, 1972; see Chapter Six). It is often advisable to have observers record their replies to questions with the help of rating scales, and not with a "yes" or "no" answer. Three-point scales are appropriate for younger students, five to seven-point scales for older students. Observers should read the questions carefully before the discussion. Several observers, each with a different questionnaire, could function simultaneously, thereby covering most of the important aspects of group process during a discussion. However, in the early stages of group learning, the teacher may prefer to concentrate on one specific feature at a time. Here are two questions from the list presented above in scale form.

1.   How much time was spent discussing irrelevant matters?

1	2	3	4	5
a great deal	a moderate amount	some time	very little time	none at all

2.   How many group members contributed to the discussion?

1	2	3	4	5
one or two contributed	only a few contributed	about half contributed	most contributed	everyone contributed

Discussants as well as observers can use simple rating scales to evaluate their own role in the discussion, and to serve as a basis for comparison with the comments of the observers. The questions presented above for use by observers serve equally well for discussants. Even one question might suffice to stimulate an instructive analysis of the group process so that discussants can improve their discussion skills (Schmuck and Runkel, 1972):

How do you feel about your participation in the discussion?

1	2	3	4	5	6
very satisfied	quite satisfied	somewhat satisfied	somewhat dissatisfied	quite dissatisfied	very dissatisfied

Observation schedules. Following are two observation schedules suggested for observers of elementary and high-school age groups (Schmuck and Schmuck, 1974). The discussants to be observed read the items in the observation schedules before the

Jot Down Initials of Students

	Time 1	Time 2	Time 3	Time 4
Task Jobs Giving Ideas:				
Getting Ideas:				
Using Someone's Idea:				

Jot Down Initials of Students

	Time 1	Time 2	Time 3	Time 4
People Jobs Being Nice:				
Saying How You Feel:				
Letting Others Talk:				

Figure 8. Observation sheet for goal-directed leadership (elementary).

Time

	1	2	3	4	5
1. Initiating: Proposing tasks or goals; defining a group problem; suggesting a procedure for solving a problem; suggesting other ideas for consideration.					
2. Seeking information or opinions: Requesting facts on the problem; seeking relevant information; asking for suggestions and ideas.					
3. Giving information or opinions: Offering facts; providing relevant information; stating a belief; giving suggestions or ideas.					
4. Clarifying or elaborating: Interpreting or reflecting ideas or suggestions; clearing up confusion; indicating alternatives and issues before the group; giving examples.					
5. Summarizing: Pulling related ideas together; restating suggestions after the group has discussed them.					
6. Consensus testing: Sending up "trial balloons" to see if group is nearing a conclusion; checking with group to see how much agreement has been reached.					
7. Encouraging: Being friendly, warm, and responsive to others; accepting others and their contributions; listening; showing regard for others by giving them an opportunity for recognition.					
8. Expressing group feelings: Sensing feeling, mood, and relationships within the group; sharing own feelings with other members.					
9. Harmonizing: Attempting to reconcile disagreements; reducing tension through "pouring oil on troubled waters"; getting people to explore their differences.					
10. Compromising: Offering to compromise his own position, ideas, or status; admitting error; disciplining oneself to help maintain the group.					
11. Gatekeeping: Seeing that others have a chance to speak; insuring a group discussion rather than a one-, two-, or three-way conversation.					
12. Setting standards: Expressing standards that will help group to achieve; applying standards in evaluating group functioning and production.					

TASK FUNCTIONS (items 1–6); SOCIAL EMOTIONAL FUNCTIONS (items 7–12)

Figure 9. Observation sheet for goal-directed leadership (secondary).

discussion begins. Students should not be observed without their knowing the aims of the exercise. One way of engaging students in practicing discussion skills is to ask each discussant to make sure that he performs one of the skills described in the observation schedule. Practice in observing is also a potential source of learning about discussion skills for the observers, no less than for the discussants.

In Figure 8 and Figure 9 the observers write the initials of the student who performs one of the skills listed. There are many possible variations which can be made in these schedules, to suit the needs of various groups. For example, an observer can be assigned to a particular discussant and the observer checks an item each time that the discussant behaves accordingly. The schedule for high school can be divided among two, three, or four observers, each one using some of the items to direct their analysis.

Chapter Six

Activity Centers and Learning Centers

Activity centers and learning centers are specific areas in the classroom where learning materials are displayed. The students spread out in the various centers, where they work in small groups or individually. The content of these centers may be determined by the curriculum or selected by the students, according to their own interests. Materials chosen for the centers contribute to the students' acquisition of basic skills, and at the same time they are free to use the materials as imaginatively and inventively as they can. They may also move among the various centers and communicate with each other. Group formation in activity and learning centers is very informal and on the basis of common interests (Barth, 1973). Thus, activity centers and learning centers incorporate the main characteristics of small-group learning. They afford opportunities for communication and cooperation among students and allow for varying degrees of initiative in the use of materials and subject matter. Moreover, centers can be planned and constructed by the students themselves.

A number of features distinguish activity centers from learning centers, and these will be discussed later in this chapter. But several essential assumptions and characteristics are common to both: these are that productive learning occurs when conditions make possible individual search and discovery; that the curriculum allows considerable flexibility in selecting subject matter; that the student's direct experience with concrete materials and situations promotes the development of abstract concepts; and that the teacher's role is to counsel and guide each student's activities.

Activity Centers: Introduction

Activity centers create a learning environment which provides pupils with a rich variety of materials. Each pupil investigates the materials in order to identify their qualities and discover their different uses. Typically, there are a number of centers in a classroom, and they are defined by some general topic, such as a reading center, math center, music center, crafts center, etc. Reading, writing, and arithmetic are learned as integral parts of ongoing activities in the various centers. Teachers and teachers' aides, who may be parent volunteers, or even some of the pupils, assist individual students or groups, who proceed at their own pace in the different centers. Thus, each student is encouraged to choose the activity which interests him and to pursue it at his own pace for as long as he feels necessary. In short, free choice of topic, variation in activity, emphasis on *process* rather than on *product*, and the teacher's role as guide are the outstanding features of the activity-center approach to classroom organization and learning.

Learning Centers: Introduction

Learning centers offer a more structured approach to classroom organization and to the students' use of learning materials. A learning center's goal is clearly specified and not just given a general title. Students engage in tasks prepared in advance by the teacher, and suited to their learning ability, so that each one can progress according to his own needs.

The extent to which students are free to select the learning center they desire depends upon the rules set up by the teacher. Participation in some centers may be required, while others can be considered as "electives." Some choice should be open to the students, even regarding the required centers, such as deciding in which center they will work and when. In classrooms where the teacher also determines the order in which the students will proceed through the various centers, freedom of choice will be limited to activities not directly related to the curriculum.

Learning centers do create conditions for discovery learning, but the discovery experience will be restricted to those materials which the teacher displays in a given center in accord with the specific learning goal. In middle and upper elementary grades, students learn to construct centers based on their interests, whether or not these coincide with the curriculum. Required and elective centers can coexist in the same classroom in such a way that the required centers deal with topics dictated by the curriculum, and elective centers reflect students' interests.

In the following pages we discuss the range of possibilities open to teachers in the use of activity and learning centers.

ACTIVITY CENTERS

Curriculum in the Open Classroom

One student reads in one corner of the room; in another, three are working on a scientific experiment; in a third, two are preparing a puppet show; and a fourth small group sits on a rug near the teacher, who is helping them improve their reading skills. Around the room are many centers stocked with stimulating materials. In some are small packs of file cards, which suggest and describe certain activities; in others, students engage in activities which they invent themselves. There are no rows of desks, no bells to mark the end of a lesson, and no teacher's desk placed at the head of the class.

The curriculum for the activity center type of classroom serves only as a set of guidelines, indicating which general concepts, content, and skills should be emphasized or which kinds of development should be encouraged. The teacher must decide which of the topics suggested by the curriculum coincide with the students' interests and, therefore, are appropriate for intensive study, and which are peripheral and deserve less attention.

While the curriculum may suggest topics which will certainly be of inherent interest to the students, it cannot guarantee that everyone will be interested in the same topic at the same time and in the same sequence. Therefore, the students should be given the chance to choose the subject which appeals to them and to work at it until they have explored most of its possibilities (Blitz, 1973).

The teacher will guide the students' activities so their work at their chosen center will be meaningful. For example, a teacher observes a group of pupils constructing a train. He or she can suggest a number of books which describe different trains which can be a point of departure for investigating a variety of subjects, such as the history of railroads, mathematical calculations regarding speed and distance, the crisis in the railroad industry due to the increasing use of air freight, etc. These topics may or may not appear in any curriculum, but the teacher uses the students' expressed interests as a means of getting them involved in their own research.

It is also possible to teach curriculum-prescribed material and at the same time allow the students freedom in selecting their learning activities. One way of doing so is to divide the time available between required and elective topics, as noted above. Another is to present a lesson to the entire class about the fundamentals of a given subject and then to let the pupils, individually or in small groups, pursue whichever aspects of the general topic appeal to them.

The curriculum should serve as a helpful guide to teachers in identifying the skills and concepts appropriately taught at given ages or grades. In addition, the teacher should have information about the students' previous learning experiences and about what is planned for future years. With this information the teacher will know more or less what range of knowledge and skills to expect among the students and to integrate these expectations with the students' expressed interests.

One of the teacher's critical functions in this setting is the selection of materials for the centers. The materials are the stimuli for arousing the students' curiosity, inventiveness, and thinking processes. As time goes on, the teacher adds or removes items on the basis of his or her observations of the students' preferences. Comprehensive lists of materials are to be found in a number of sources (Blitz, 1973; Stephens, 1974; Weber, 1971).

Open classroom organization maximizes the responsibility the students assume for their own studies (Rogers, 1970). First of all, they must select from an array of materials those items appropriate for the topic they have chosen to study. Then they must decide how to use them. Initial attempts to use the materials already constitute a learning experience. The students must touch the materials, examine them, manipulate them, try to join different items, listen to or smell them, and perform various experimental acts in an attempt to understand their various characteristics. The teacher may intervene at the point where the student is ready to deduce principles and arrive at higher-level understanding based on his own experiences. By assisting students in relating one experience to another, the teacher helps them arrive at some generalizations. This process is the essence of concept formation.

Clearly, therefore, another important function of the teacher is to guide students in planning their activities. A student may become so enthusiastic about the materials he is working with that he sets himself unrealistic goals. Consultation with the teacher will often help him recognize this and set appropriate goals.

When students adjust to thinking of the teacher as an advisor and guide, they become more active in the learning process and their work improves. Gradually they engage less in trial and error and are eager to learn the skills needed for solving problems with learning materials. Proficiency in the use of materials enhances the pupils' independence. They are already making the transition from experiences with concrete objects to systematic problem-solving.

Children acquire the fundamentals of writing, reading, and mathematics during their investigation of the available materials. The way in which these subjects are integrated in the students' activities deserves some elaboration.

Writing. The open classroom promotes spontaneous communication among students. By showing a personal interest in each student's comments, the teacher eliminates his or her "judging" role and the tension it produces. These conditions are critical for stimulating students' innovative and creative efforts. In such surroundings, learning is relaxed, pleasurable, and gratifying, and students eagerly share their ideas and reactions (Hassett and Weisberg, 1972).

Direct contact with materials gives rise to a host of verbal reactions. The children want to describe what they see, feel, and discover.

Recording experiences with materials in activity centers is a natural extension of students' original activities. One of the most consistent impressions reported by observers of the activity center type of classroom (or "open classroom") is the remarkable quantity of writing done in contrast to the amount usually produced by students in the traditional classroom (Blitz, 1973; Hertzberg and Stone, 1971; Rogers, 1970; Weber, 1971).

There are many ways of involving students in writing activities. Some written products, such as comments on art works, structures, or photographs of wild life, can be displayed on bulletin boards or as explanatory aids near objects. Others might be placed in hard binders and put in the class "library." These notebooks are for future study, and their number grows during the year (Hassett and Weisberg, 1972).

Teachers may decide to give each student a notebook in which to record his impressions, stories, descriptions, or even the new words he learns to spell. Knowing that he may later have to copy sections of his notebook for his classmates, the student will have a strong motive to write legibly and pay attention to spelling. Before his work can be put on the bulletin board, he must copy it without spelling mistakes; he may use a dictionary, or get help from classmates or the teacher whenever he is in doubt about spelling.

Even if a pupil's written work will not be displayed before the entire class, it should be corrected. However, it is best not to interrupt the flow of communication, and to postpone corrections until the pupil comes for individual consultation with the teacher. The teacher can then use the pupil's own writing as the basis for instruction in principles of spelling and writing. If two or three students make similar mistakes, they can be grouped together for an hour on one or two days to learn or review the necessary rules. The point is that the conventions of writing and spelling are taught *as needed* and not according to an arbitrary, pre-determined schedule (Hertzberg and Stone, 1971).

Reading. Books are naturally included in the materials found in activity centers, and there is also a library or reading center, containing books on many different subjects and reading levels. The students are in fact surrounded by books. Teachers read to them and they also write their own stories and books and read them to each other. The various activities also lead them to books to seek information. In the lower elementary grades, for example, cards can be placed in the centers identifying the names of objects in the classroom, such as doors, closets, and blocks (Weber, 1971). Reading on many levels is thus integrated naturally with the other activities found in the room.

There is no one book from which children first acquire their knowledge of reading. Early reading skills are learned directly from their experiences and activities. The teacher writes some title which a child used for a painting, or writes down a story told by one of the students. Children thereby begin to read words related to their own experiences, images, or fantasies. Reading topics are not *assigned* to pupils. Rather, the wealth of topics which they mention themselves is exploited in order to create occasions for reading, which are at once absorbing and instructive.

Learning the alphabet and other skills required for analyzing words also stem directly from the child's activities, and are not a separate subject. The teacher who knows several different ways of transmitting these skills can select the one most appropriate for a particular student. In reading, as in all other areas of learning, an individual approach seeks to adapt methods and materials to the pupil's age, interests, and abilities (Hassett and Weisberg, 1972; Hertzberg and Stone, 1971; Weber, 1971). As with writing, a few pupils who need practice and support in certain skills can be grouped until they reach their goal, whereupon the group is disbanded.

Mathematics. The abundance of materials in activity centers provides an infinite number of opportunities for pupils to develop their mathematical concepts. They have many occasions to weigh and measure objects, and can have experiences related to conservation and to grouping items conceptually. Much equipment used for calculations is found in the mathematics center, but this does not mean that experiences relating to mathematics are restricted to one center. For example, when students build something, they may have to recognize and measure geometrical forms. When cooking, they must measure and weigh quantities of food. Even painting a picture poses various problems of measurements and proportions (Weber, 1971). Hertzberg and Stone (1971) offer many excellent suggestions for activities to develop mathematical understanding.

Learning mathematics need not be confined to particular hours of the school program, nor isolated from the rest of the pupil's experiences. It is not necessary to invent artificial mathematical problems, because students encounter genuine problems requiring mathematical solutions in most of the activity centers. Many occasions will arise for practicing measuring, counting, and calculating. The sequence of teaching found in the traditional mathematics curriculum can guide the teacher in devising appropriate materials to enrich the students' mathematical discoveries (Hassett and Weisberg, 1972).

Other subjects. Materials placed in the activity centers should be effective media for learning about a wide range of subject matter; geography, nature studies, history, etc. Children's curiosity about their environment leads them to activities and discoveries which cut across boundaries between different subjects. For example, while pupils are engaged in what appears to be a mathematical task, they may suddenly find they are doing something more akin to a scientific experiment. While measuring food quantities for cooking, they ask questions about the changes which occur in food as a result of temperature changes, and about the difference between the food before and after cooking (Weber, 1971). These experiences contribute to the student's general scientific knowledge and to the development of a scientific vocabulary, which helps them describe their experiences adequately.

For purposes of convenience, the range of the students' activities can be divided into general subjects. These subjects are not identical with the *subject-unit* in the traditional classroom. In the activity center type of classroom, the subjects have greater breadth and their study is not limited in time. Rather, the connections *between* subjects or disciplines are emphasized, stressing the basic characteristics common to all scientific thinking.

The fundamental approach to subject matter in the activity center is to present a broad topic, such as "Air," "The Planet Earth," "Careers," or "Pollution" (Hertzberg and Stone, 1971; Stephens, 1974). In order to develop these topics, the teacher selects materials which stimulate the students to conduct individual or small-group research. The investigation of these topics is frequently carried out by small groups, formed by pupils with common interests. Each group is responsible for planning the method of its investigation, the type of summary it will present, and the duration of the project (Stephens, 1974). It should be noted that research projects conducted by small groups are a typical component of the open classroom.

Activity Cards

The teacher guides the pupils' learning by suggesting new problems for study. At times, teachers may suggest possibilities for solving problems and recording the results of their work.

One way of guiding activities is for the teacher to prepare a set of "activity cards" (Hertzberg and Stone, 1971; Weber, 1971) to distribute among the appropriate centers. They contain suggestions for tasks and activities for pupils to work out either in small groups, using techniques described elsewhere in this book, or individually. The suggested tasks are planned so that they will reinforce concepts which the students acquired through direct use of materials. Or, the cards may suggest an entire sequence of tasks intended to develop a basic understanding of a concept. These tasks open up new possibilities for experiments and discoveries which enrich the activities devised by the students themselves.

During the course of the year the teacher increases the number of activity cards. The tasks which he or she proposes should stem from his or her observations of the interest which students show in particular activities. Students may also add their own cards. Examples of card sets are offered by Hertzberg and Stone (1971).

How to Begin

The transition from a traditional classroom to one organized in the form of activity centers should be gradual. Pupils and teachers may plan together the pace at which they will make the transition, based on how they react to the initial changes they introduce into the classroom.

Blitz (1973) notes three ways of changing to an open or activity center type of classroom. According to the first, the teacher changes the structure of one lesson so that the pupils work individually on the tasks they have set. The lesson begins with a short class discussion in which the topic is presented. The class clarifies what the pupils know already about the topic and also what they would like to learn about it. Immediately following this discussion, everyone proceeds with related activities, individually or in small groups, investigating different aspects of the topic.

It is important to provide materials which will actively involve even the more aloof or disinterested students. For example, the teacher begins by explaining the concept of three-dimensional measurement. He or she then suggests that the pupils construct three-dimensional structures from blocks and record the structures' measurement. Another example might be the characteristics of a magnet: after discussing some basic principles, the pupils put different-sized magnets into practical use.

This way of getting acquainted with the open classroom does not require any change in the seating arrangement or the placement of the desks in the room. The day's activities are still divided into the conventional subjects. It is during the "open" lesson that students have their first experience of self-directed research.

In a second approach to instituting an open classroom the teacher chooses a general topic and the students select sub-topics to investigate. The teacher's role is restricted primarily to providing the materials needed to pursue the work fruitfully. He or she should avoid giving directions. One corner of the classroom is turned into a center for the study of a given topic, and all the appropriate materials are concentrated there. This "corner" of the class can be a table, a bookcase, a cupboard, or just some shelves. Students at first acquaint themselves with the materials in any way and any order. During this time they will probably ask many questions which will point to possibilities for further research of interest to the students. At this point, it is important not to answer the questions directly. Instead, they should become the starting point for the pupils' own research, eventually leading them to the answers.

Finally, a third suggestion for changing to open-classroom learning is to set aside one hour a day for "free study," unrelated to any specific subject or academic topic. Students are free to occupy themselves in any activity they choose, but this hour should not be used for play alone, and this may happen if the classroom does not offer a variety of materials which stimulate investigation and discovery. Two or three activity centers should be stocked with materials relevant to several subjects. A variety of materials provides different qualities of tasks, and appeals to the interests of different students. Some pupils will want to work alone, others in small groups.

Reading is an appropriate activity for the free hours. Some teachers fear that pupils will not achieve the proper reading level this way, but in fact reading practice is best acquired through individual or small-group work, because there is rarely one level of reading in any classroom. A "reading center" can be set up, containing books at different levels of complexity and on a wide choice of subjects. Even books containing mainly pictures can be included. Each student picks the book which attracts him, and the teacher does not interfere with this choice. Some students examine one book together, others read to the teacher, and still others read alone.

The free-time period can be expanded once students become accustomed to choosing their activities and accepting responsibility for their studies. Skills learned during free-choice time should be applied gradually to different topics, until the entire day is conducted as one continuous session, no longer divided into subject periods.

The teacher moves among the different groups and observes

how the students pursue their tasks, what materials they choose, what activities they perform with their materials, what groups evolve among the students, how well they concentrate on their work, and whether the materials arouse their curiosity. These and similar observations must be made with the greatest possible objectivity, without criticism, and without obvious direction.

Record-keeping. Keeping records about children's activities starts with the transition to the activity center type of classroom and continues throughout the school year. These records tell which materials should be added to the existing collection and which should be eliminated (perhaps temporarily). Each student also keeps his own record, including his compositions, drawings, and other written work.

In the intermediate grades of elementary school, where students can plan fairly long-term activities, the diary might include space for recording activities for major subjects on each day (Hertzberg and Stone, 1971; Stephens, 1974).

Evaluation. Open education emphasizes the process rather than the product of learning. Instead of a product-oriented method of measuring achievement, the teacher records the child's manner of dealing with tasks, his learning behavior, his interests, and activities. These records help the teacher to follow the child's development in terms of his ability to concentrate on extended activities, to plan learning experiences, to interact with classmates, and to feel secure in a relatively unstructured environment. The record of the teacher's observations will reveal at a glance who needs encouragement or advice and who can proceed unaided.

One of the most effective and instructive ways of evaluating a student's work is to meet with him individually and regularly. These meetings deepen the relationship between teacher and pupil. The conversation can touch on the student's interests, his activities, problems with a current project, or his relationships with classmates. In this relaxed and friendly atmosphere, one can also learn if the student has any difficulty in understanding concepts or acquiring skills. If so, the teacher can suggest an exercise from one of the activity cards, or teach the student what he must know during their meeting. Or, the teacher can note this student's difficulty and later form a group of students with similar problems in order to correct them (Hertzberg and Stone, 1971; Weber, 1971).

A class must have fairly frequent discussions about the way it operates, as well as about what it studies. These discussions can clarify many issues which are critical for effective learning in this type of classroom, such as how pupils move around the room; what materials are needed in various centers; or how to place the centers in different parts of the room. Group cohesiveness will also be enhanced by having everyone contribute to formulating classroom policy. To accomplish this, some teachers have short group discussions at the end of each day or each week.

LEARNING CENTERS

Learning centers enable the teacher to devise tasks suited to different levels of ability and to a variety of interests. Every center offers one or more tasks which improve students' knowledge of a subject, or increase proficiency in a specific skill. The subject matter or skills presented in the learning centers can complement the topics being investigated by small groups.

Generally, only a portion of the school day is devoted to work in these centers. Learning centers can be integrated with other teaching techniques, including the different types of small-group learning described in this book. In one classroom, for example, a few students may work individually or in pairs at several learning centers, while two or three small groups continue their research projects, and yet another group meets with the teacher. The students rotate through the various types of activities so that, over a period of time, all of them will have participated in all the forms of learning available. Another way of integrating a variety of learning techniques is to set aside specific sessions for improving skills or for seeking information at learning centers and devote other sessions to small-group research. At times the teacher may wish to address the class as a whole.

Types of Centers

Following are descriptions and examples of different types of learning centers, with their particular characteristics and goals.

Center for improving single skills. Students seeking to improve mastery of a particular skill work individually in this kind of learning center. Before working alone, the student participates frequently in a group seesion or in a full-class lesson. In the first two grades, for example, a center may appear as in Figure 10.

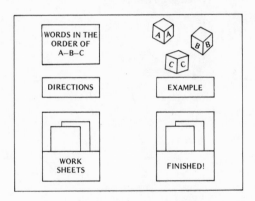

Figure 10. A learning center.

The "center" is a large section of cardboard or construction paper with a sign indicating its goal. Other items hung on the board are:

- A page with the following instructions and explanation: "The letters of the alphabet appear in a certain order. On your work sheets write a list of words in alphabetic order."

- A pocket on the board contains the work sheets. Each student working at this center takes a work sheet and completes the task written on it. When he finishes, he returns the sheet to the pocket.
- The teacher collects all the sheets, corrects whatever is necessary, and places them in the child's personal file.

A second or third pocket can be added to the center, containing sheets for more difficult tasks. Students may choose tasks at whatever level they wish, but they should perhaps be urged to try the easier ones first.

The center depicted in Figure 11 reinforces one skill by three tasks (three sets of work sheets).

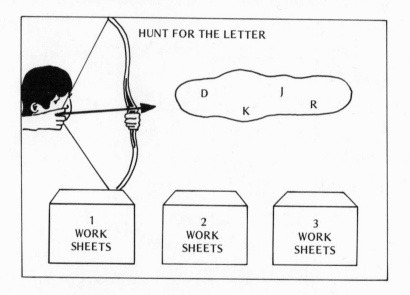

Figure 11. A single-skill learning center.

All the tasks found in this center strive to improve students' ability to recognize the first letter of words. Students work in this center after acquiring the basis for this skill in a small-group or full-class lesson. In each pocket on the board, students find cards on which pictures and work sheets are pasted. Several letters are printed on each work sheet. Instructions for filling out the work sheets are pasted on the outside of the pocket.

Learning centers for developing distinct skills can help students learn all the skills they need in order to study a given academic topic. These skills might include use of a dictionary, proper usage of punctuation, matching pictures to sounds, reading maps, or basic arithmetical skills. A skill must be divided into smaller components, and the teacher can then construct a learning center for reinforcing these specific components. Of course, not every student needs to work in such centers, only those who need help in the specific skills.

Multi-skill centers. The tasks at this type of center require students to employ more than one skill. For example, the specific skills may be visual and auditory discrimination. In the pockets attached to the board are cards with pictures pasted on them, and the name of the figure in the picture is printed on the back of the card. Pencils, crayons, and paper are found on a nearby table. A list of instructions for the students is also attached to the board, which might include the following:

- Take a card from one of the pockets.
- Match the pictures which have names that rhyme.
- Draw the pictures with rhyming names on the paper provided.
- Write the appropriate name next to each picture you drew.

The teacher checks if each pupil "hears" the rhyme.

Multi-skill centers in the intermediate and upper elementary grades help students develop a variety of research skills. Each center contains tasks which involve practicing such skills as consulting a dictionary; using an encyclopedia; reading a map; consulting periodicals; using different kinds of indices; locating sources of information in a library; and distinguishing between important and irrelevant information.

The following center illustrates one way to help students to practice these skills (see Figure 12).

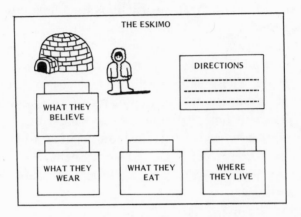

Figure 12. A multi-skill learning center.

The goal of this center is to develop research skills at an appropriate level for the class. Instructions for students are:

• Choose a research topic (food, clothing, housing, or religion).

• Write a story about or a short summary of the selections you read.

• Draw a picture to illustrate your story or summary.

Books and other relevant sources of information are found on the table on which the "center" is placed. Students may also be directed to other centers where all the books are concentrated. They will then remain at this Resource Center until their project is completed (Voight, 1971).

To evaluate pupils' progress, the teacher meets with them individually or with a small group that has worked at a particular center. Each one reads what he wrote and a short discussion follows.

Project centers. Learning centers are remarkably suitable for use within the framework of unit teaching. Teachers who wish to organize the unit around learning centers can construct a number of centers in the classroom, each devoted to one content area. The centers are planned according to the sequences appropriate for the particular unit. In this way, they may be placed according to a determined order. The first one presents a broad view of a topic through pictures and other materials which attract attention, arouse curiosity, and raise questions leading to further study. Additional centers contain tasks which teach students how to search for information, at the same time as obliging them to use various learning skills. These tasks also enrich their general fund of concepts (Voight, 1971).

The enrichment center. Activities at this center are not directly related to curricular studies, but are based upon important concepts and skills. Typically, these activities stem from students' interests which are expressed spontaneously in the classroom. The center is created by cooperative planning; together students decide what activities are to be included, their number, and their goals. First, the group planning a center consults with the teacher, who helps them structure their ideas. The students' own enthusiasm can often interfere with their planning. It is advisable for the teacher to edit the pupils' suggestions, if necessary, and guide them in defining their goals.

An enrichment center might be constructed related to a holiday or some community event. The anniversary of the founding of the community in which the school is located might motivate students to put up a learning center for investigating local history. Two or three tables joined together, with pieces of cardboard placed on them, form the center. A title is printed toward the top of the cardboard, and pictures are pasted on it depicting scenes from local history. Students might write letters to some of the community's senior citizens, or invite representatives to tell how the community was built. It may even be possible to build a model of the community—or part of it—at some period in the past, based on early pictures, maps, or verbal descriptions. The "town history" center can become a stimulus for extensive research when coupled with these kinds of activities.

An animal raised in the classroom can also provide impetus for setting up an enrichment center. Next to his cage (or aquarium) are directions of how to care for his needs. Pupils divide responsibility among themselves for fulfilling these tasks.

Diagnostic centers. Tests used in this center survey students' knowledge in subjects such as reading, arithmetic, and other basic skills. The purpose is to assess each student's level of functioning in that subject. In fact, the survey is an informal diagnosis with teacher-made tests. There is no doubt that the student's total productivity in school should be the basis for evaluating his educational needs. However, from time to time the need arises to examine learning difficulties more closely. This is critical when a student fails repeatedly to master an important skill in the normal course of his learning activities. The teacher then directs the student to the diagnostic center to do one of the survey tests which can locate the weak points in his performance. Students know that the evaluation will help *improve* their learning, and is not meant to *prove* whether they know something in particular. On the basis of the information from the survey, the teacher decides what activities would best overcome students' weaknesses. Students should be involved in evaluating the results of the test and in planning the remedial activities.

The diagnostic center is stocked with a rich variety of exercises printed on cards. A set of cards, with exercises arranged in a developmental sequence, concentrates on the skill needing practice. A diagnostic center is thus very similar to a skill center, and cards from the latter can be saved and used in the former. In any case, the cards from these centers should be filed and used whenever the need arises.

In the lower elementary grades, diagnostic centers contain, for example, exercises which check pupils' knowledge of the alphabet, phonics, and simple addition and subtraction. To assess reading level, the teacher might prepare short passages taken from a variety of books in the classroom, and provide a few questions after each to check comprehension; one or two questions assess the reader's understanding of details, a third question probes his ability to "read between the lines," that is, interpretative ability. These questions may be written, or, preferably, asked by the teacher during consultation with the student.

The sets of cards are placed in pockets, each one of a different color indicating the subject of the card-set (red pocket for reading cards, green for arithmetic cards, etc.). If the room is large enough, several diagnostic centers can be set up; one for reading, another for arithmetic, another for study skills.

Prescriptive centers. Students are directed to the prescriptive center after their basic learning skills are assessed in the diagnostic center. Activities for improving weak skills appear on work sheets or cards found in the different-colored pockets (similar to the color-key used in the diagnostic center). Pupils usually work individually in the prescriptive center, but those who have already mastered a particular skill can help a classmate who still needs practice.

The prescriptive center can be a permanent remedial station in the classroom. Those needing help for extended periods can have a fixed time set aside every day for work at this center. Special activities will have to be planned. Appropriate materials might be available commercially. These activities are not related to topics presented at other centers, but are based only on the developmental sequence of the skills requiring remedial help (Voight, 1971).

Independent learning center. Students working individually or in small groups prepare these centers. They determine the goals, plan the activities it is to include, and then carry them out. The teacher advises the students only when asked. Students who did not participate in planning the center may still perform some of the activities in it.

It may happen that pupils suggest various kinds of independent centers which do not seem practical. These suggestions can be recorded and filed in a special card catalogue of suggestions. Perhaps it will be possible to realize some of the ideas at a later date. In this way a "library" of ideas for different kinds of centers can be built.

Independent learning centers operate without teacher supervision and without their content being dictated by the curriculum. But these centers are valuable educationally. Students learn a great deal, engage in creative activities, and get much satisfaction from their efforts. They must also cooperate in planning and constructing the center. On occasion, an independent center becomes an enrichment center. Also, if students show interest in putting up a center which deals with one of the subjects they are studying, their independent learning center can be added to the centers originally set up to teach the particular subject. In that case, all of the students in the class will carry out the activities in the independent learning center.

Designing Learning Centers

Motivation. A center should be colorful, have an inviting caption or title, and be constructed to attract attention. This can be achieved simply and need not strain the teacher's or pupils' imagination or talents. The way in which the title is written, the colored construction paper covering the cardboard, the way the table is covered—all these create a pleasant and attractive center. Photographs, pictures, and objects relevant to the topic also add interest. In the intermediate and upper elementary grades, learning centers are more complex than in the lower grades, and informational materials are emphasized. This information gives students an introduction to a topic and involves them in carrying out various learning activities connected with it (Baker, Ross, and Walters, 1971; Cote and Gurske, 1970; Voight, 1971).

Specific learning goals. Every activity offered at a learning center must derive from a specific goal which the teacher formulates. The goal may be stated in the center's title. For example, a center designed to improve students' acquaintance with the map of the world bears the title "A trip around the world," which requires them to identify places on the map. Looking over the center as a whole will also emphasize its learning goals.

Clear formulation of a center's goals is prerequisite for checking if students have achieved these goals. A teacher must do the following:

1.   Define the specific learning goal of the center, such as knowing the alphabet, locating certain cities on the map, or learning two alternatives for solving an arithmetical problem.
2.   The teacher composes exercises or tasks by which students can demonstrate their mastery of the information.
3.   The results of the students' work must be checked to evaluate their performance.

If a choice of activities is offered, they must all lead to the desired goal.

Instructions. Directions to students must be as short and clear as possible. Some centers have two kinds of instructions: one set is displayed openly, another appears on work sheets. The instructions displayed on the cardboard are more general, such as: choose an easy work sheet (or a harder one, or a red, or green one), fill it out, and then read a chapter in a particular book. On the work sheets appear only those instructions related to the particular task.

Components of a Center

Learning centers may take various forms, the most common one being a large piece of construction paper or thick cardboard bearing a title and sheets or cards which provide instructions for learning activities. This cardboard is set up on a table or attached to a blackboard, bulletin board, wall, or the side of a bookcase. An imaginative variety of centers is depicted in detail by Cote and Gurske (1970) and by Voight (1971).

Work sheets. Each work sheet contains a clearly defined learning activity, an example of how to carry it out, and space to write a report or reply.

The work sheet described below is fairly complicated. It proposes a number of activities from which students may choose. This work sheet belongs to an enrichment center set up near a center whose theme is protecting the environment. Activities listed on these sheets can be carried out by individual pupils or by small groups, in either the intermediate or upper grades of elementary school.

How to Protect the Environment

Choose three activities from the list below, and carry them out, either alone or with two or three of your classmates.

1. Locate and read four articles dealing with the protection of the environment. Summarize these articles on one page, including at least three facts in your summary. On a separate page record the name and date of the newspapers and the pages on which the articles appeared.
2. Draw a poster about preserving the landscape. Use materials found in the crafts center.
3. Prepare an experiment which illustrates the destructive nature of air or water pollution. Record the experiment—its goals, procedures, and results—in your notebook.
4. Write a letter to a society which is trying to protect the environment, and ask for any information they distribute free-of-charge. Prepare a display from these materials.
5. Prepare a five-minute lecture in which you try to persuade your class to help safeguard the environment, prevent air and water pollution, and protect natural resources.

This work sheet could serve as a "center" by itself. It would be tacked up on the wall or put in an envelope bearing a title together with other work sheets on the same subject. The envelope would be placed near a center where students study basic facts about that subject (Cote and Gurske, 1970).

Cards. Directions for activities often appear on cards. This is especially convenient when several steps are required to carry out a task. A card "catalogue" is formed describing an entire sequence of activities.

One card can contain all the information necessary to complete a given task. For example, the following card is one of a set dealing with computation skills:

Measure the distance from Point A to Point B on this card. Write your answer below.

A ————————————————————————————— B

distance_____

Another card tells a student to perform an activity which requires a sheet of paper and other materials:

On graph paper make a diagram of the school on a scale of *1 square = 1 yard*. Calculate the distance between the entrance to the building and the door of your classroom.

If there is no room to erect learning centers on tables or in corners, the card catalogue can serve as a "center." Small file boxes of different colors can be placed on a table, each with a title describing its contents, and they become a series of learning centers. A student picks one or two cards, goes to his work area to carry out the instructions on it, and returns the cards to the box when he is finished.

File. A center may be made out of a folder, an "accordion" file, or any other convenient container to hold the necessary materials. The activity is defined on a card attached to the file or folder. Since the folder is portable, students can work on these tasks anywhere in the room. The colors of the folders identify their subject matter, such as green for chemistry experiments, red for arts and crafts (Cote and Gurske, 1970).

Bulletin board. A bulletin board is a convenient place for a learning center because the display can be changed easily. Everything usually found in a center can be combined on the board: a title, informational materials, pockets containing work sheets, and so on.

Small cardboard boxes or envelopes can be tacked onto the bulletin board. These contain different materials needed to carry out the activities on the instruction cards. Two round paper plates can be formed into a pocket by folding one plate in half and pinning it on the lower portion of the other plate.

Objects or learning aids of all kinds add variety and interest to a center. They are usually placed on a table beneath the bulletin board.

How to Begin

To achieve a smooth and gradual transition to a classroom organized around learning centers, the teacher might begin with single-subject centers, while other subjects continue to be taught in the customary way.

At the start of the students' work at learning centers the teacher explains the nature of the activities found in the various centers. The class is then divided among the various centers and allocated activities. At this stage the centers may be no more than colored boxes containing instruction cards or some kind of tasks. The boxes, each with a title, are placed on a table, and the students can take a task to their seats or to some specified place in the room.

One suggestion for the lower elementary grades (Rogers, 1970) is that all the centers be devoted to one subject. Thus, for example, if the topic is magnetism, each center will contain a magnet and several objects. All the pupils will have a chance to use the magnet on objects made from various materials and to learn, through trial and error, which objects are attracted to the magnets. They record their observations and make the proper inferences. This task is short and has clear goals, which makes it an appropriate way for pupils to become acquainted with the learning-center approach. At the conclusion of the activity, it might be helpful to hold a class discussion to clarify what transpired.

Another approach would be to set up centers dealing with different tasks, but all related to the same subject (Cote and Gurske, 1970). In one center pupils could experiment with magnets and a variety of objects, while in another they could form various figures out of metal shavings and magnets. In still another they could read about magnets, or perform other experiments with them. The class divides up among the various centers. After completing the task at one station, students move on to another. Once students become accustomed to the learning-center approach, they themselves may choose the center at which they wish to work.

When the novelty has worn off and students learn to move from one station to the next, this technique can be introduced into the study of many subjects. The entire school day may be spent at different centers, or the day may be divided between study at centers and other techniques. Different techniques may be used during the course of the same lesson (Voight, 1971). Thus, for example, the teacher might convene the entire class at the beginning of the day and explain a particular principle about the topic. Then students will go to different centers and carry out activities related to what they heard earlier. These tasks may last several days. The teacher moves among the centers, helps students who have difficulty, and also meets with groups or individuals to see how they are progressing. When everyone has finished his activities, the class meets again to summarize its findings.

Changing the Centers

A direct or indirect approach to changing a center may be used when it is no longer useful (Voight, 1971). A direct approach means that the teacher convenes the class, tells them about the change, and explains the purpose and procedures of the new center. An indirect approach would be when the teacher sets up a new center, and pupils, individually or in small groups, find out themselves (with some help from the teacher, if necessary) how to use it.

The amount of time to be spent at a center can be decided in advance by the teacher. Setting time limits helps students organize their school day, but these limits are not to be imposed rigidly. A pupil who needs more time should continue to pursue his activity at a center without undue pressure. In fact, pupils who rush through their activities should be reminded that quality is preferable to speed. With these qualifications in mind, it is still potentially helpful to set up a reasonable time schedule.

Record-keeping and Evaluation

Each student keeps a file of his completed work sheets. But teachers must still make a note of students' movement from one learning center to another and keep track of their experiences in the classroom. A suggestion for a record sheet follows, but teachers should prepare record sheets appropriate to their own teaching goals. It is advisable to keep the number of record sheets to a minimum to avoid being overburdened with paperwork.

Recording Students' Choice of Stations

A large placard can be pinned to a bulletin board on which pupils indicate at which learning centers they completed their activities. This system helps students to keep track of past work and to select their next center. The placard may be divided according to the centers operating in the classroom.

Each student has several cards with his name on them, one of which he tacks under the name of the station at which he is working. If he works at more than one station during the week, his name appears in more than one column.

Under the name of the center, the teacher might wish to write suggested time limits on work at that center.

In addition to this "class schedule," each student keeps his own record of the stations at which he studies, the dates, and his own evaluation of his work. This evaluation is usually made after a consultation with the teacher.

A supply of record sheets should be prepared in advance, and in lower elementary classes, a new sheet distributed to students every week. If upper-grade students are able to plan their work well in advance, their record sheets need be exchanged only once a month.

When it is desirable for students to keep more detailed records—as, for example, with those who are very young or those who are just making the transition to the learning-center approach—the record sheet can be a daily record of a student's work.

The name of the center can be prefaced by the general subject it covers, so that it can easily be seen which subject areas each student has studied: for example, "Reading—The Library," or "Nature Studies—Migration of Birds." In this way, the student's personal record sheet gives a clear picture of his learning activities. Teachers can also refer to these sheets when discussing the pupil's progress with parents (Hertzberg and Stone, 1971; Voight, 1971).

Recording Skills

A different record sheet can record the acquisition of learning skills and concepts. These records are kept by the teacher, who fills them out after a consultation with the student.

When a student masters a certain skill or grasps a new concept, his achievement can be indicated under the name of the appropriate learning center. These skills and concepts are the goals of the learning centers in the classroom, so this list exists—at least in part—even before students begin their work at the centers. But many concepts and skills may emerge during the students' activities which the teacher did not anticipate (Voight, 1971).

Evaluating the Centers

Evaluation must be extended to the centers and not focus exclusively on the students. It is important to know how much interest a center generates, how clearly defined its activities are, and to what extent students could carry out these activities independently or in small groups. Most important of all is the extent to which the center's learning goals coincide with the pupil's achievement. After completing activities at a center, the teacher tries to ascertain, during individual or group consultations, if the student has learned what the center intends to teach. The teacher should avoid conveying to students the idea that their learning at the center must consist of specific details and ideas. Such rote-learning would defeat the purposes of the learning-center approach, which tries to stimulate pupils' curiosity and research. The teacher should also try not to force the student's learning into a precast mold; the object is to *understand and analyze concepts*, rather than amass quantities of details. The nature of the evaluation process will exert great influence on the way students utilize the centers. By constantly evaluating what students have learned from a center, both teacher and students can help improve the centers and make them more stimulating, interesting, and helpful (Blitz, 1973; Voight, 1971).

Evaluating Adjustment to the Centers

Students in the learning-center classroom must develop cooperative work habits and self-discipline, since they are not constantly in the teacher's presence. Voight (1971) suggests that it is advisable to observe their behavior in several areas as in the evaluation scale described below.

Evaluation Scale for Student's Work at Learning Centers

Select one number from this 5-point scale for each of the following questions:

low   1   2   3   4   5   *high*

1. level of work habits
2. ability to complete tasks within the stipulated time limits
3. ability to follow directions
4. level of participation in setting up learning goals during consultations with the teacher

5. degree of self-motivation
6. extent of participation in group activities at centers
7. ability to work without disturbing others
8. does student offer help to others when necessary?

Individual Consultations

Regular meetings with individual pupils are an essential part of the learning-center approach. These meetings give the teacher an opportunity not only to estimate the student's progress, but also to learn about his approach and attitude to his work at the center. Together, teacher and student review the record sheets and work sheets and discuss any problems the student has in dealing with the materials. The frequency of the consultations depends upon the students' needs; some require more support from the teacher than others. But the teacher-pupil consultation must, at all times, foster free exchange of ideas, encouragement, and constructive assistance. Turning the consultation into a miniature examination will impair the learning centers' chances of success. It is better to avoid a fixed schedule for meeting with students, to retain maximum flexibility, and to view the consultation as a means of meeting individual learning needs (Hertzberg and Stone, 1971; Voight, 1971).

Guidelines for Selecting Materials

One way in which the teacher can discover what materials arouse the pupils' curiosity is to bring an initial selection of materials to the classroom so that students can begin work immediately. Observing their activities, noting which objects they use and how, and discussing their interests with them will provide the teacher with a basis for enlarging the collection and getting the students involved in learning activities. This procedure is appropriate for the lower grades. In more advanced classes the teacher can circulate a questionnaire or ask students directly what kinds of objects they would like to examine. Any object which arouses pupils' initial interest can be a useful starting point for learning.

Activity and learning centers both give students a chance to manipulate objects, and to discover their many features and functions. Before presenting materials to students, the teacher should try them out as if he or she were one of the students and record his or her own associations while handling the materials. These notes will help produce provocative questions or challenging activities for students to investigate, as well as give him or her ideas for choosing new materials. After students have had a chance to get to know the materials and try them out, they meet with the teacher to discuss all the research possibilities presented by them. From these discussions can arise suggestions for activities and research projects for individuals or small groups (Hassett and Weisberg, 1972).

There are several sources of useful materials for the centers. Many schools have collections of old objects in forgotten corners of the building which can often be brought back into service. Students can be asked to bring discarded objects from their homes. Factories and workshops often have a surplus of goods they can no longer use. There are also many materials which the students themselves can construct (Glasser, 1971).

Chapter Seven

Role Playing

Introduction

Teaching methods which encourage cooperation among students cannot ignore problems in human relations which are bound to arise. Students must be helped to develop sensitivity to each other's needs and to communicate effectively, so that group learning may be productive (Smith, 1966). Collective decisions must be made with a degree of empathy for the values and views of others. From one point of view, learning in groups may be seen as a series of situations which require the constant clarification and solution of problems in human relations. True, some academic task may be the central focus of the group's activity, but the group nevertheless tries to cope with the task by means of a social process. This process of communication and cooperation in planning and performing learning tasks is itself one of the major components of the learning experience. Failure in group relationships means failure in the ability to learn as a group. It is highly advisable, therefore, that constructive relations, which will contribute to the group's cohesiveness and cooperativeness, should be planned and not merely left to chance. Preaching about the virtues of cooperation will not help students learn the social skills necessary to becoming effective group members. In previous chapters we presented techniques for promoting constructive relationships and effective participation among group members, including listening games, the use of observers during discussions, and cooperative planning. Another major technique for learning to solve problems in human relations is role playing (or sociodrama).

Role playing is a largely spontaneous dramatic activity usually performed by a small group of persons whose goal is to explore some problematic social encounter, an exploration intended to provide both participants and observers with a learning experience. The experience should increase their understanding of the human feelings, perceptions, and acts involved in the situation under observation and contribute to their ability to behave more effectively when similar situations arise again. The dramatic presentation likens the experience to a real-life encounter so that actors do not rehearse parts or learn scripts in advance. There is only a short planning session at the start in which the basic features of the setting are determined, such as the problem in question, where and when the encounter takes place, and the identity, age, and position of the characters involved.

Role playing is not intended to be a means of improving the players' acting, or of imparting factual knowledge, though some facts may be passed on as background for the presentation. It is rather a spontaneous dramatization for the purpose of clarifying human relations (past, present, or future) in terms of their social, emotional, and cognitive implications. Role playing can help participants clarify the *how* and the *why* of people's behavior toward each other (Corsini, 1966; Nichols and Williams, 1960; Shaftel and Shaftel, 1967).

This clarification emerges because the spontaneity of the dramatization allows for a fairly open expression of one's ideas and feelings in response to the behavior of other players. The players are supposed to speak their thoughts and feelings on the spot, as if they were the person whose role they are playing. Because the players are not required to recite specific lines or answer specific questions, and are not representing themselves (which would transform role playing into psychodrama), they can feel less inhibited or anxious about expressing their feelings than they would in a more formal setting. This makes the role play an enjoyable, releasing experience, not unlike the feeling of wearing a mask and saying things one might not normally say.

However, it should not be forgotten that role playing is intended to contribute to learning and therefore should include a cognitive component also. The more intellectual part of the play comes into effect after the dramatic episode ends. All players and observers analyze and discuss the play, including the thoughts, attitudes, assumptions, and feelings of the players, as they were portrayed. After an understanding of the implications of the play's roles and relationships has been arrived at (specific steps in this process are discussed later in this chapter), the observers are asked to suggest alternative behavior in the same situation. These suggestions can be used as the basis for a re-enactment by the same or other players.

Some Implications of Role Playing

The ability to put oneself in another's place requires of us that we perceive some of the other person's qualities and interpret them to ourselves. Some of these qualities are evident, but others are covert. They include needs, motives, abilities, and ideas. When people deal with each other, their interactions are influenced by the ability to understand each other's qualities. This process of "role taking" occurs whenever people try to understand each other, and their behavior toward each other can be powerfully influenced by this understanding.

Three different approaches to the educational significance of role taking have been considered by different authors, and each illuminates another facet of this complex process. They are: (1) the cognitive-communication approach, based on the work of Piaget and his disciples (Feffer, 1959; Flavell, 1968; Piaget, 1926); (2) the affective-social approach, based largely on the work of Moreno and his students (Moreno, 1946, 1953); and (3) the approach to role taking as a process of social learning (Maccoby,

1959). Each of these schools of thought deepens our insight into the potential significance of role playing as an educational tool, particularly when students are working with others in small groups.

1. **The cognitive-communication approach.** Piaget and those influenced by his work describe the conversation of very young children as lacking a communicative goal. Indeed, their speech cannot be accurately described as real verbal communication, and these young speakers behave as if they assumed that they can read each other's minds without being required to express themselves in a manner comprehensible to their listener. During his development, the child maintains many social contacts and learns to adopt different points of view about experience. Thus, he gradually emerges from the intellectual egocentrism typical of the very young child and develops powers of reasoning by which he can examine events more objectively. When his understanding of himself and his environment is more objective, based on his expanded understanding of other people's ideas and not only on his own thoughts, it is more likely that he, the speaker, will be able to adapt his spoken messages to the needs of his listener. When the speaker cannot properly assess how the listener thinks and feels, they are likely to conduct two separate monologues, with their messages to each other conveying only occasional meaning (Flavell, 1968; Lin, 1973; Piaget, 1926; Sarbin and Allen, 1968).

Experiments have been conducted to study the extent to which children's ability to take another's role influences their communication with each other. Do they pay attention to the knowledge available to the child with whom they are speaking, in order to direct their own flow of information? Or, does their speech perhaps have little direct meaning for the listener? Will their exchange lead to a real flow of shared meaning? All these questions have been asked, and research has shown that our ability to take on the roles of others determines in no small measure our ability to express ourselves informatively in conversation. Role taking develops over the years. Very young children are largely unaware that their perceptions and concepts are one-sided and do not take other person's informational needs into consideration. This cognitive egocentrism is reflected in their limited ability to take on the roles of others and to formulate their messages accordingly (Feffer, 1959; Feffer and Gourevitch, 1966). It seems likely, therefore, that encouraging children to take on the roles of other people, at least in a dramatic setting, and to communicate with others as if they were someone else, could improve their communication skills.

2. **The affective-social approach.** Given that our behavior toward others is influenced by our intellectual understanding of them, it would follow that improving that understanding will influence our attitudes. The affective-social approach to role-taking emphasizes the need to understand varying attitudes, values, and feelings as a basis for improving relationships among people of different ideological, cultural, or social backgrounds. This approach views role taking as a potentially powerful instrument for achieving social goals. The assumption is that giving students repeated role-taking experiences will help them cultivate greater sensitivity toward and understanding of other people; this change in attitude could equally result in a change in behavior. Of course, everyday life offers a multitude of opportunities for role taking, but people are generally unaware of such experiences.

Role playing offers a technique for the explicit development of positive social attitudes. Students are able to practice their behavior in various problematic situations, free of anxiety and criticism, so that they can learn to cope with the situations and solve the problems. Role playing has many advantages, one of the greatest being the possibility of going back and re-enacting the situation without hurt feelings and no responsibility for mistakes being felt. The circumstances can be recreated with the aim of improving behavior and acquiring more effective social skills.

Because of this particular quality, role playing has been called "reality practice" (Chesler and Fox, 1966; Corsini, 1966; Haas, 1949; Hendry, Lippitt, and Zander, 1947; Lippitt and Hubbell, 1956; Shaftel and Shaftel, 1952, 1967).

3. The social learning approach. Observations of children's behavior have shown that they frequently act in ways typical of other people whom they know or have observed, and they appear to be "playing" the roles of parents or other adults. During this play the children imitate the adults so that the children's behavior is more typical of the adults than it is of children. Moreover, children act these roles not only when they are with other children but also when alone and are not aware of being observed. The role taking seems to develop their ability to understand adult behavior toward them, and in this way, the children can rehearse fulfilling the expectations of the adults in their environment.

This self-training through play contributes to greater harmony with adults, as well as preparing children for their own future roles in various social situations. Also, it cannot be assumed that children learn to behave like their parents or like other adults only by having observed them; the practice gained in play helps to reinforce these behavior patterns on a very fundamental motor level, and brings the children's actual behavior closer to that of the adults whose roles they take on (Maccoby, 1959).

All of the above approaches to the explanation of role taking lead to the conclusion that developing a deeper understanding of another's role is an important educational goal, and that role playing seems to be one of the primary techniques available for fostering this kind of understanding. By creating the opportunity for children to behave like someone else—to express that person's ideas and feelings and to relate to others in the way he might relate to them—role playing greatly helps to develop understanding. When "pretending to be someone else," people permit themselves freer expression than their own inhibitions would otherwise allow them. The experience also opens the gate to greater self-understanding and to awareness of the relationships involved in the role play.

If a student sees a variety of behavioral solutions to a situation depicted in role play, he might become better able to make decisions about relationships. This is made possible by the personal and emotional dimension which role playing adds to learning. Even if the subject of the role play is of typical academic content, derived from some literary, historical, or political situation, the spontaneous dramatization brings the topic close to the student's life and involves him.

The impact of spontaneous role playing can perhaps be explained by saying that it bridges the gap between thought and action, a gap characteristic of most formal learning situations, in which learning is almost exclusively on a verbal level, divorced from feeling and movement, rather like Hamlet's answer to Polonius' question: "What are you reading, my Lord?" Hamlet: "Words, words, words."

The desirability of linking thought and action more closely is consistent with Piaget's theory of mental development, according to which human knowledge is not a reproduction of reality recorded by man in machine-like fashion. Nor are concepts acquired by mere reception of information through our senses. In Piaget's view, concepts are acquired in the wake of environmental transformations which we bring about ourselves. We construct, in an intellectual sense, the concepts which we learn through our own manipulation. Action is therefore the basis of knowledge. Abstract intellectual acts, which Piaget calls "operations," are rooted in more fundamental sensory motor acts (Piaget and Inhelder, 1969). Learning through role playing involves a high degree of unity of thought, feeling, and action. This multi-level experience makes it a potentially powerful and instructive experience for the student.

When to Use Role Playing

Role playing is a versatile technique appropriate for use in a

wide variety of situations. First and foremost, we urge frequent
use of role playing to clarify problems arising from the applica-
tions of small-group teaching techniques in the classroom. This
should help students find constructive solutions to their problems.
Used in this way, role playing is more than just another of the
small-group teaching techniques, but actually facilitates the
practice of these techniques. Thus, for example, role playing can
be used to show students how to serve as committee chairmen, to
lead a discussion, be coordinator of a research team, or work out
problems of students' participation in learning groups. The
problems of the domineering or shy student, or issues of
cooperation and competition, can also be explored through this
technique, and it may be particularly helpful in making the
transition from a more traditional type of classroom to one
organized into small groups. It will also give students an
opportunity to acquire various skills which will help them feel
comfortable in the new situation.

Role playing is particularly effective when used as an integral
part of a curriculum, and not merely as a one-time experience—a
kind of dramatic interlude in the regular routine. It should be
woven into all of the approaches to group learning presented in
this book. It could be used as a method for summarizing a group's
research effort, or for acquiring skills needed for the conduct of
research.

While no attempt will be made here to list all possible topics
for specific role plays, it should be stated that it has been used
frequently in social studies, on all grade levels from elementary
school through university. Social studies include such subjects as
citizenship, political science, cultural geography, economics, urban
studies, and many more. In all of these, role playing can
contribute to the clarification of human relations. A few specific
examples might include:

- conflicts arising from social inequality;
- an investigation of the influence of social and historical

events on life adjustment, such as in immigration and/or adaptation to a new country, city, or school;

- a scene including a customer and a clerk or salesman, or a relationship between a professional and his client, e.g., architect and home-owner, doctor and patient;
- development of sensitivity toward the behavior patterns of different cultures; inter-ethnic conflicts—causes and solutions;
- acceptance of responsibility as a citizen for community problems; and
- an interview for a job.

These topics and many others can serve effectively as background for role playing, particularly when investigated by students before the play session and when the role playing complements other learning techniques. Many background scenarios for role-playing sessions are provided by Shaftel and Shaftel (1967).

The school can contribute greatly to improving ethnic relations, a problem presently confronting many nations. Students can investigate issues troubling communities. Using group methods, schools can help students do research into the historical, economic, and social backgrounds of their communities, and analyze the causes and development of their problems. Role playing can assist students to understand the problems and cultivate a feeling of involvement with the community. It can also help make the students feel that they share responsibility for the future of the community and that they can assume an active position toward these problems, rather than examining them solely academically.

The use of role playing is not limited, however, to social studies or to the clarification of social problems. It has also been used for teaching literature (Graham, 1960; Hoetker, 1969; Magers, 1968). In drama education, for example, teachers have noted that for the student to develop an appreciation and interest in art, it is not enough for him to be brought into contact with the great works of art; he must also be helped to understand that drama is an expression of man's condition, and be able to relate it directly to his own needs and feelings (Hoetker, 1969).

Through role playing, students can develop a measure of personal, emotional, and intellectual involvement in the characters in a work of literature. When dramatizing these characters, it is important to emphasize the spontaneous aspect of the role play. Players should not be asked to reproduce a plot as it unfolds in the original story. If a role is entirely planned, it becomes drama, not role playing. Students should be encouraged to improve their own story-endings or to alter the plot according to their view of the particular role they are playing. They may act out alternative solutions to the written relationships. The "legitimacy" of these proposed solutions when applied to the character as portrayed by the author could become a subject for discussion in the post-play analysis. In some cases, such an approach can reveal weaknesses or inconsistencies in the author's development of a character, and students have occasionally suggested more successful, profound, or life-like solutions than those offered in the text. Role playing can also encourage students to read a text more carefully and critically than they might do otherwise, as they have greater motivation to understand the characters they will portray.

Spontaneity is equally important in the role playing of historical events and personalities. It is recommended that students act the roles of fictitious persons in particular historical situations rather than those of famous people whose histories are already well known, as this knowledge would color the acting with preconceived ideas, thereby inhibiting spontaneity. Students can base their role play on knowledge of a particular period, place, or set of events, and still leave room for spontaneous improvisation. One teacher asked his students to read a book up to a particular page and no further. Role-playing sessions were then held in which a variety of solutions were suggested for the situations described so far in the text. Only after the students had role played their own solutions, did they finish reading the text and compare their results to the actual events (Graham, 1960).

Role playing has been used for a wide variety of purposes, including teaching language skills (Perry, 1950), anthropology (Sayre, 1957), concepts in physical health (Greenberg, 1961), family relationships (Wood, 1970), special education for the retarded (Blackhurst, 1966), and changing attitudes of emotionally disturbed children toward school (Harth, 1966). Research evaluations of role playing were summarized by Mann (1956) and by Elms (1969).

Criteria for the Use of Role Playing

The appropriate use of role playing, as we have already pointed out, is determined mainly by the nature of the situation in question, rather than by any specific subject matter. To assess whether a topic is suitable for role playing we can ask ourselves a number of questions, the answers to which should all be positive. If any one answer is definitely negative, then some other technique would be better suited to dealing with the topic (Chesler and Fox, 1966; Shaftel and Shaftel, 1967).

1. Can role playing this particular topic achieve the following:
    a. arouse a lively discussion after the play?
    b. increase students' understanding of the feelings, viewpoints, and values of other group members?
    c. examine possible implications of people's behavior in certain situations?
    d. help observers to understand the attitudes and behavior of persons in the roles presented?

2. Are the observers sufficiently knowledgeable about and involved in the problem to be depicted?

3. Are the setting and details of the problem sufficiently clear and straightforward to allow dramatic portrayal within the short time usually allocated for role playing (generally a few minutes)?

4. Are any players likely to remain peripheral to the role play?

5. Can the appropriate conditions for role playing be created in the classroom, or in some other room in the school?

6. Does the role play have clear goals? .

7. Are there students in the class who will play the roles willingly, and without being "pressured" to volunteer by the teacher or anyone else?

8. Will the role play deal with problems of human relations which are of general concern and do not relate to any particular student? Will the play avoid hurting individuals?

Steps in Preparing for Role Playing

Students will find role playing more satisfying and instructive when the necessary preparations are made for it to proceed in an organized fashion. The following eight steps can serve as a fairly comprehensive guideline for conducting role playing:

1. selecting the topic and preparing the class;
2. choosing actors;
3. determining specific background details and providing some general sketch of the roles to be depicted;
4. training the audience to observe with specific aims;
5. the role-play session;
6. players and observers discuss the role play;
7. re-enactment of the role play, based on alternatives suggested during the discussion;
8. evaluation of the implications for behavior in other, comparable situations (generalization).

Let us examine each step in detail.

1. **Selecting the topic and preparing the class.** Either the students can choose a topic themselves, or the teacher can do so and try to emphasize its significance for the students. The students should certainly be encouraged to suggest their own topic, but this might be postponed until after they have had at least one

role-playing experience. It is crucial, however, that the topic should have direct bearing on the students' life experience, so that they are aware of its relevance, whether intellectual or emotional. It is advisable to have the students themselves point out in what way they consider it relevant, and this should be done during the preparatory phase. Students cannot be expected to become involved in roles or interpersonal encounters with which they feel no affinity and in which they will be unable to empathize with the feelings and thoughts portrayed.

When the teacher is convinced that the students appreciate the topic's relevance to them, then the more concrete aspects of the setting can be determined. These concern the immediate physical environment of the encounter and the problem involved, and they greatly influence the behavior of the players. The description of the situation can be relatively short, but it must be credible and interesting, and care must be taken to ensure that it is realistic and does not portray any idealized notions of "man's nature" and his relationships. Such idealization would almost guarantee that students will go through the motions of role playing because they are expected to, but it would be no more than another academic exercise with which they cannot identify.

Often a short story or portion of a story, or a newspaper report, offers important details about some meeting which would be suitable for role playing. Perhaps, the students themselves might be asked to write a story or news report to provide background material. The story would best be left unfinished, and the aim of the role play would be to portray possible conclusions. Reading an unfinished story and asking students to suggest endings can arouse interest in the subject and draw students' attention to specific details to consider in formulating their conclusions.

By and large, a student's proposal should not be rejected as inappropriate without careful explanation of the reasons for its inappropriateness. Any suggestion which bears some reasonable relationship to the circumstances of the story or to the qualities of the roles should be considered and investigated.

2. **Choosing actors.** When forming acting groups, it is worth considering the possibilities of dividing the class into two or more role-playing teams, each group with its own actors and observer-audience. This division, of course, depends on the space available in the room being used. Conditions permitting, therefore, a class of 30 students could be divided into three teams of ten members each, of whom two, three, or four students could first take the parts of actors, and the remainder of observers, with the roles alternating during "the team's" progress through the role-play sequence. The different teams could choose to role play the same topic, different aspects of the same topic, or distinctly different topics. In any case, the portrayals, and consequently the later discussions about them, will differ from one group to another. It can be an enlightening experience for students to hear and compare what took place in each group. If all teams decide to portray the same situation and cooperate on planning the setting, then similar reactions are sometimes heard afterwards. On occasion, however, one team's original portrayals will be the source of an analysis which has not occurred to any other team.

Actors should be volunteers and should express a reasonable interest in their roles. Some people think it preferable for an actor to identify thoroughly with his role; however, though such involvement can sometimes be an asset, it is not a prerequisite for a successful portrayal. Nevertheless, the student's desire to play the role and his interest in it—which can be estimated in the class discussion prior to the role play—are certainly more decisive criteria in the selection of actors than considerations of his acting ability. The latter, in fact, need not figure at all in the production or assessment of role playing. Similarly, care must be taken not to choose actors whose services have been volunteered by others on their behalf, perhaps for reasons of popularity. The students should be genuinely interested in performing the roles. Moreover, there should be opportunities for most, if not all students, to take a role at some time, so that a wide variety of roles should be offered in the course of time. The teacher will have to provide moral support for the more reticent students when their turn comes. It is to be hoped that these students will, after the initial ice is broken, be more willing to play other roles in the future.

3. **Determining background details.** There is no script to learn, and players do not rehearse before the performance. The preparation of a script or determination of specific acts in advance would eliminate spontaneity. The planning stage consists of setting general guidelines for the scene: a few words to describe the location (such as a yard behind a house, a living room, or a small grocery store) and a general description of the opening action to help get the scene under way. The unfolding of the scene occurs entirely as a result of the actors' reactions to each other in keeping with their grasp of the roles.

4. **Training the audience to observe the role play with certain goals in mind.** Active audience participation in the post-play discussion is a vital element in the whole sequence and, without it, the play will not achieve its goal. The observers must be coached in advance in order to ensure a productive discussion so that they do not view their task as one of criticism or imposition of irrelevant goals on the role play. Their attention should be focused on the nature of the human encounter portrayed by the actors. One of the goals of role playing is to develop the students' ability to concentrate on various features of social behavior with a degree of empathic understanding for another's situation, whether they agree with it or not.

The observers should be influenced by the total impression of the role play rather than merely of the individual players. Moreover, no individual player should be criticized, but only the *role* which he portrays. True, an actor portrays a role as he sees and understands it, but it is important to distinguish between the person acting and the role being acted, and to help students understand the difference between them. It should be clear that the actor is playing a *role*, not himself, and the *role*, not the actor, is what the observers want to understand.

Furthermore, since the quality of the acting is not an object of evaluation, actors should not be praised or criticized for how well they acted. The criteria for evaluating the portrayal are: to what extent did it portray the situation as described in the initial guidelines; what were the thoughts and feelings expressed in the scene; and did the experience provide an opportunity for "reality practice" for both actors and audience?

Members of the audience can be given specific tasks to perform, such as concentrating on a particular role, or a specific aspect of the interaction between actors, or finding answers to questions such as: "What would you feel in this situation?" "What would a person's feelings be as portrayed—at the start of the scene, or at the end of the scene?" After the observers have had some experience with role playing, they should be able to suggest alternative solutions to the one actually presented, and these can become the basis for re-enactments by a different set of actors.

5. **The role-play session.** At this stage comes the actual portrayal of the scene, as authentically and spontaneously as possible. The scene should evolve as a result of the actors' reactions to each other's acts and comments, and to the feelings expressed in the play situation. They must also try to understand the feelings of the persons whose role they are playing and mold their portrayal accordingly. This means that the role play should evolve as a chain of reactions while the actors try to act according to the role requirements, but without conforming to any explicit plan, beyond the general guidelines, which might restrict their portrayal.

The feeling of spontaneity must equally be extended to the actors' language. They must not feel obliged to use their "best" vocabulary if it is not in keeping with the role, or should a local dialect be used if the roles belong in a different locality or historical period. Part of a realistic portrayal is dependent on the language, so the actors should speak as uninhibitedly and realistically as possible lest the entire role play lose its authenticity.

Sometimes, students overcome their inhibitions only after many experiences of role playing. This may be particularly true of students accustomed only to a traditional classroom, as they may be quite unused to performing spontaneously, free of the idea of satisfying the teacher's expectations of them. Freeing the students' spontaneity in thought and action may require much practice, although that may seem rather a contradiction. During the first role-play experiments, teachers should expect students to get "bogged down," not to know how to continue, their speech halting and marked by embarrassing moments of silence, and their action blocked. Trust in the teacher's support and knowledge that he or she will neither sanction nor criticize, together with the acquisition of greater skill through practice, will gradually increase students' competence (and confidence) in role playing.

How many actors should participate in a role play? Obviously, there is no set answer to that question. To give each actor a chance to contribute to the dialogue when there is no script may perhaps require limiting the number to three or four. More experienced students can still perform well with five actors. The students' age should be considered here; those in the early elementary grades generally perform better with only three participants. The teacher will have to experiment with different-sized groups to find what is the best number. Of course, the background story itself will be a determining factor.

How long should a role play last? Again, there is no standard answer, and much depends on the nature of the acting and the age of the students. With younger pupils, 15 minutes may be enough for both the role play and the following discussion. If the presentation is particularly successful—which means that the play is proceeding with spontaneity and the discussion is lively and productive—there is every reason to allow it to continue to its natural conclusion. It has been known for students in junior and senior high school to perform a role play for an hour each day during an entire week, until all of its possibilities were exhausted.

The central guideline is: Allow the role play to continue until some clarification of behavior has been achieved. Discontinue the play when there is an adequate basis for a discussion, when the players and audience seem to have learned something from the presentation, or when they have had ample opportunity to practice a specific skill.

6. **Discussion and evaluation.** The first to speak immediately after the role play should be the players themselves. They should tell the others about their own thoughts and feelings as they performed their roles, and should also give their opinions on thoughts and feelings expressed by the other actors. In other words, each actor should explain his view of the others during the scene and what prompted their particular behavior.

It is interesting to compare the players' and the observers' evaluations, the latter usually having a great deal to say. Incidentally, if the more timid students do not contribute, it might be a good idea to suggest that the next role play deal with ways of encouraging everyone to participate in the discussion. Students accustomed to a lot of seat work may need practice before participating freely in discussion.

In the discussion, students will examine the meaning of the scene portrayed, the relationship between all the roles, the cause-and-effect relationships between the actors (or their roles)—all without identifying any specific role with the actor as a person. The teacher could encourage students to describe similar situations in their own lives, suggest alternative solutions, and analyze the conclusions they arrive at from the role play, and their implications, in contrast to the conclusions suggested by the alternative solutions. This type of discussion aims at developing the students' understanding of the causal nature of behavior and its consequences.

The guiding of the discussion can be successfully accomplished with open questions, such as: "What did so-and-so feel in that situation?" "What happened afterwards?" "What do you think are some of the possible consequences of so-and-so's behavior?" "Could such a thing happen to you?" "Why not let the observers, who saw the play from a different point of view than the players, tell us their evaluation of what happened in the role play?" The players should also be free to suggest new solutions during the discussion, or new ways to improve the role play. In short, the post-play discussion involves all participants, players and audience alike, in an effort at solving problems of human relations; it also sets the stage for a replay which will try to overcome a particular problem more effectively.

7. **Re-enactment.** We noted that role playing is a form of "reality practice" which is an opportunity for the players to practice solving problems of human relations in a neutral environment without the fear of any real consequences to their acts. The consequences are all hypothetical anticipations of what could happen as an outcome of certain behavior. It therefore appears desirable to give students the opportunity to repeat role-playing situations several times, if circumstances are favorable, so they really can "practice" behavioral skills and not rest content merely with the theoretical comments made during the post-play discussion. Favorable circumstances mean, primarily, the level of student interest in the role play, the availability of interesting proposals for alternative solutions, and a lively post-play discussion. As long as students express interest in the topic and continue to reveal hitherto unexplored aspects, there is every reason to replay and re-analyze the situation. The goal of role playing, after all, is to make students appreciate the complexity of human behavior, and the more opportunities they have to analyze an episode, the more alternative viewpoints will have a chance to emerge.

There are no predetermined time limits to the post-play

discussion; it can last several minutes or an hour. As long as it continues to progress and does not become repetitious, it need not be interrupted. Lively and interesting discussions can be terminated prematurely by school bells or by the beginning of a study period for another subject. If such abrupt endings can be avoided, all the better.

8. **Evaluation and generalization.** In some cases, after one or more role-playing sessions, it will be possible to come to general conclusions which apply to social situations other than the specific one portrayed. Such general conclusions will usually suggest themselves only after a series of episodes has been presented and only when the nature of the presentation provides a suitable basis for such conclusions. Pupils in the early elementary grades are frequently unable to formulate general statements verbally, particularly since the learning of the role play is not completely verbal. They may have learned important lessons from the role play without being aware of them on a verbal level, but only on an action-behavioral level. Of course, the teacher can aim at formulating the play's implications verbally but it would seem unwise to press too hard in this direction.

Guiding the Play

Role playing is based on the assumption that the students themselves must discover the implications of the relationships presented. The discussion is the primary factor in this learning process; in it the students try to analyze the play logically and understand and identify the behavior of the actors and their solutions of the issue at hand. The assumption is that the "discovery" approach will make students more personally involved in the role-playing process and, hence, emphasize the relevance of the learning experience to their own lives. These assumptions imply certain guidelines for the teacher's attitude during the role-playing sequence.

First of all, teachers are advised not to assume a specific

moral position or express any personal opinion about the problem or any one solution to it as portrayed in the role play. Even if the teacher personally disagrees with the solution presented, it should be borne in mind that role playing is a means of exploring human relations, not judging them. If students present a socially unacceptable solution, the teacher should not try to "teach" the more "correct" solution by simply stating what it should be. In the role-playing situation, the teacher's moral judgment is best suspended to allow the students their own evaluation of behavior in the play. They must gradually come to distinguish between reasonable and unreasonable, effective or ineffective solutions on the basis of peer interaction rather than the teacher's intervention as an authority figure. To paraphrase a saying of Piaget, if we "teach" (i.e., tell) the students the "correct" solution, we might prevent them from learning it.

The teacher could certainly intervene, criticize, or offer suggestions if extremely negative, vulgar, or aggressive behavior is displayed, but this is exceedingly rare.

There is a real danger that the *students*, rather than the teacher, will demand conformist patterns of behavior from the actors, and will give moral criticism to the actors without trying to understand the roles portrayed. Students are liable to misinterpret the distinction between actor and role as separate units. The teacher must defend the actors from their classmates' criticism, and help observers to understand these important distinctions. Students must feel quite confident that they do not have to seek the teacher's favor by criticizing or by making any other comments which, although they may not even believe in them themselves, would, in their estimation, agree with the teacher's or the school's professed values. The observers' attention should, as far as possible, be drawn away from the actors as people, and toward the social, *inter*-personal aspects of the role play. The actor's right to portray a role as he sees it must be protected, even while emphasizing the observers' responsibility to suggest alternative interpretations and portrayals.

Teachers might wish to make comments in this vein: "Why do you think James understood that role as he did?" "What can we learn from Susan's presentation of this role?" "Ought we to ask the actors to portray these roles as *we* see them?" "Perhaps you can explain to us what you feel (or think) about the matter?" The point of such questions is to help the audience create more "distance" between themselves and the actors as individuals and so encourage a more objective evaluation of the roles portrayed.

The guidance of role-playing sessions requires teachers to focus their attention on the students' comments and to try to think *with* them instead of *about* them. The main problem for the teacher is what they are trying to express. In effect, the teacher has the same problem as the audience in any role play, which is to try to identify with the roles portrayed in order to understand what the actors are trying to say. It is to be expected that the teacher's capacity for empathy and analysis is superior to that of the students so that, by questioning and drawing students' attention to certain features, the teacher can help the students achieve greater understanding. This type of questioning is partially "reflecting"; the teacher reflects the students' feelings and thoughts back to them so they can see them more clearly. Students may not even be aware that their comments on their fellow-students' acting reflect their expectation that others should think and behave as they wish. Having such feelings reflected indirectly and in an atmosphere of support can help some students achieve a new degree of maturity.

Becoming Accustomed to Role Playing

Students can get used to role playing gradually. Sometimes, particularly with younger children, simple practice exercises can be helpful as a preparation for more complex episodes. Some authors (Chesler and Fox, 1966) have suggested the use of pantomime as a means of introducing role playing. Individual students could perform the movements of someone walking in mud, stepping in a pile of marbles, walking barefoot on hot sand, eating a hot potato, a lemon, or a hot pepper, brushing his teeth, dressing, removing a speck of dust from his eye, and so on. These should all be performed without speech.

After this initial round, two pupils might perform simple acts together, still in pantomime form, such as pretending they are playing ball or throwing pieces of ice to each other. A mock telephone conversation is an enjoyable and effective way of introducing speech into the exercises. One of the participants could be given certain information, for example, that he has to go to the dentist, or is invited to a party, or a friend is asking how to get to his house from some distant place.

After this simple practice, students can be asked to portray each other. For instance, a small group can select a topic for a short discussion. After some minutes, the teacher interrupts to tell the students that, in a moment, they will be able to continue the discussion for another ten minutes, but for the time being each of them is to take on the identity of the person sitting to his right, and to talk and behave consistently as if he were that person. The students announce their new names, and the discussion proceeds.

A final set of practice situations is having two students present very short plays. One tries to copy from the other when he should be doing his own work; they could "fight"; they cooperate on a school task (preparing a map, play, or science experiment); a student who has always lived locally greets a newcomer to the school; boy meets girl. These situations have relatively simple solutions, with few alternatives.

The next step would be the portrayal of situations with the possibility of several and more complex solutions. As background for the episode, the teacher might use the interrupted-story technique. During the first few role plays, he may wish to intervene when the acting falters and ask clarifying questions, such as: "Where are you now?" "What have you done so far?" "What is the character being portrayed feeling and thinking now?" Such probes force the actor to define his location, the time of the event, or other circumstances of the role. "What kind of person are you playing?" "What would such a person do now?" "Try to ignore the audience and do whatever comes to your mind now!" Help like this can renew students' courage to continue the episode.

On occasion the play does not falter at all, in fact quite the contrary. Rather, there is *too much* action, in that players talk at the same time, speak too long, don't let others take their turn, and don't react to each other's behavior, but just go along their merry way, impervious to what the others are doing. Far from arousing concern, this kind of performance is preferable to the stony silence that overcomes "inhibited" groups of students. The observers will be quick to point out the deficiencies in the actors' behavior, and the replay is almost sure to show improvement.

Role Play in the Context of
Small-Group Teaching

In our conception, role playing emerges from a broader learning effort in the class, and is not an event isolated from the study program. We have indicated that role playing can be used effectively to improve skills needed for the learning *process*, (i.e., how students work together) rather than simply being a technique for exploring *content*. In both cases, it is an integral part of the class activity, rather than a departure from it, though, of course, it can be and is used separately, as a study in human relations. We are suggesting, however, regarding it as one of many techniques in the small-group approach to classroom organization.

A unit of study for small groups which could include role playing might be devoted to the ethnic composition of the population of the United States (or any country with diverse ethnic groups, such as Israel, the Soviet Union, Mexico, England, or Canada). Research groups and discussion groups would investigate a host of the issues involved, such as the conditions under which various people immigrated to the country, what their problems of adjustment were during their first few years there, what organizations existed for aiding immigrants and whether people of common origin settled in particular geographical areas of the country. These subjects and many more can be subdivided into topics for research, dramatizations, exhibitions, etc., by small groups of students. Role playing can be used systematically as part of this overall study to explore the many complex issues of human relations which were—and are—a major factor in the life of immigrant or minority groups. But whereas the research or even the discussions can deal with broad issues, the role plays should focus on quite specific ones. The setting and problem to be presented must always be defined so that they can be portrayed within the confines of a few minutes of spontaneous acting. For example: A Vietnamese boy's first day in a U.S. school; a new immigrant from Italy goes into a Post Office; an English-language class for Spanish-speaking adults.

We shall examine a topic of this kind and follow it through the steps of the role-playing sequence.

A New Student in Class: Exploring Ethnic Relations Through Role Playing

1. Selecting the topic. An exploration of ethnic relations among students can be initially approached indirectly when a new student from a minority group appears in the class. One possibility is that the newcomer's acceptance into the class might be the subject of a discussion, with the new student participating in the discussion group. This will highlight the real relevance of the topic for class members in particular and for their community in general.

2. Choosing actors. Students will suggest specific ways of creating a pleasant atmosphere of acceptance for new students, and these can be used to make a short role-play tryout to precede the main episode. The roles played will include two "new" students and two of much longer standing in the class. These two introduce themselves to the newcomers and invite them to take part in some class activity. After this introductory run, the entire class is divided into pairs, of which one plays the "host" student and the other the newcomer. This exercise is merely to introduce their roles to each other, but role play in pairs can help prepare them for the more complex episode, as well as giving many students a chance to play the newcomer.

3. Deciding on setting and roles. The location for this episode is easily described because it is the classroom itself. The time setting is the first day of class after the summer vacation. During the first few trial runs, the new students in the class will be of the same ethnic background as the veteran students, and they presumably all live in the same neighborhood. After students have become acquainted with some of the problems of the acceptance of newcomers, they will then be able to investigate the more difficult topic of a new student from a minority ethnic group.

Students can choose the roles they prefer. Several can be members of a greeting committee; others will volunteer to help new students take part in games on the playground during recess. The teacher might have to urge students to volunteer to act the roles of the newcomers, which will be less popular. When all the actors have been assembled, they will have a few minutes to discuss their general plan for the role play, such as where they will sit or stand, and, particularly, who will open the dialogue. (This can be a decisive factor in ensuring that the role play gets off to a good start; a hesitant opening speaker will not lead to an active discussion.)

4. Preparing the audience. All students not taking roles should have specific tasks as observers. If there is a large audience, tasks can be divided among small groups. One group might be asked to concentrate on actors playing veteran students, another on the newcomers. The goals of the observation should be clearly defined, such as: (1) to note what emotions are expressed by particular actors; (2) how does the behavior of certain actors affect that of others; (3) how do the observers understand the actors' thoughts during the role play; and (4) what additional proposals can the observers put forward for facilitating the newcomers' acceptance.

5. **The role-play session.** The first atttempts at a role play are likely to be abortive. Players and observers can help each other improve the presentation and portray the situation more realistically. Portrayal of the situation from different points of view will also cast light on various problems in the relationship between veteran students and the newcomers.

6. **Discussion.** Immediately upon conclusion of the play scene, the actors and observers voice their impressions about the role playing, and alternative solutions to the encounter are proposed. If the teacher feels that the students are ready, he or she might suggest that, in the replay episode, the new students being welcomed into the class represent a minority ethnic group. Students can discuss the problems, feelings, and behavior which might be expected to emerge in these conditions. Sketches for the roles to be portrayed in the new episode will be based upon the comments made during the discussion.

7. **Replay.** The re-enactment of the episode with mixed ethnic groups obviously will be more complex to portray than the earlier scenes. The actors will represent specific ethnic groups, but it is inadvisable for minority group students to represent their own group. It would be too difficult for them, and for the audience, to maintain the important distinction between the actor and his or her role.

Before beginning the replay, both actors and observers should review the details of the setting and the roles: veteran students meet with newcomers to the class. The new students belong to a (specified) minority group. The students talk about ways to help the newcomers be accepted by the class and to feel at home in their new school.

8. **Evaluation and generalization.** Evaluation of the role

playing focuses on the audience as well as on the actors. The actors are evaluated by students and by the teacher during the discussion phase. Evaluation of the audience is frequently performed by the teacher. Two topics the teacher may wish to include in the evaluation are: (1) the extent of the observers' interest in the role play, as evidenced by their behavior during the play scene and during the post-play discussion; and (2) how well the observers analyzed the role play and provided the actors with constructive comments and suggestions for a re-enactment. Finally, groups of students can discuss how the conclusions reached during the role play may be applied in other situations in which young people from different ethnic backgrounds meet each other.

Chapter Eight

Simulation Games

Introduction

Many educators and psychologists have drawn attention to the influence of play experiences on the emotional and intellectual development of children (Herron and Sutton-Smith, 1971; Piaget, 1932, 1951), yet only recently have we begun to explore their influence on the learning process. Educational games display some of the main features of small-group learning which have been emphasized throughout this book. In this chapter we will examine one of the most promising developments in the field of educational games—simulation games.

There are many kinds of non-simulation learning games. Some teach new information, others help students rehearse certain skills, such as reading games (Wagner and Hoiser, 1960) or games to develop perceptual-motor abilities (Cratty, 1971). Our purpose here is to present a social-humanistic approach to classroom organization and school learning, and we do not presume to cover the teaching of specific subject-matter. Hence, we will not discuss games aimed solely at teaching subject-matter or skills. This does not mean, however, that we consider other kinds of educational games unworthy of attention. Small-group learning is centered on the development of cooperation among the students. Games which require players to work together in pairs or small groups (such as when classmates check each other's progress) foster cooperation and therefore make a valuable contributon to the class atmosphere.

Shirts (1972) has contributed a helpful outline for classifying games and simulations. He puts seemingly diverse activities, such as games, role playing, or films, into three major categories, and distinguishes between simulations, contests, and games, as follows:

Simulations. A simulation is anything which models reality, and can include such widely differing phenomena as mathematical formulae, role playing, films, or sculpture.

Contests. The essence of a contest is the element of competition. An election is a contest, but not a game nor a simulation. Also, there are many forms of play which are games, and are enjoyable for both players and onlookers, yet contain no element of competition. Clearly, contests can be quite distinct from simulations or games.

Games. A game is "an activity in which people agree to abide by a set of conditions in order to achieve a desired state or end" (Shirts, 1972). We have already noted above that not all games are contests; likewise, they need not be simulations, and there are many which have neither a realistic nor a competitive element.

Thus, each of these three activities can exist independently of the others. They can also be combined with each other in many ways, but we shall not explore here all the possible combinations. Suffice it to say that the activities ordinarily known as simulation games are actually a combination of all three categories, and may in fact be classified as Simulation-Game-Contests. They model reality, the participants agree to abide by a set of conditions, and they usually involve some elements of competition, so that there are winners and losers at the end.

The situations modeled in simulation games are usually social processes of some kind, frequently involving people in decision-making in order to achieve their goals. A game cannot be as complex as the reality on which it is based; therefore, a scaled-down model of that reality should be the basis of any such game. The more salient aspects of the situation must be included in this model so that the simulation will come close enough to the actual situation and give the players some sense of real involvement (Abt, 1968, 1971; Boocock and Schild, 1968; Inbar and Stoll, 1972; Livingston and Stoll, 1973). The designers of the game must decide which essential aspects of the real world to incorporate in the "microcosm" which is the game. It is this "microscosmic" quality which allows participants to manipulate the procedures typical of such a situation, and to experience some of the consequences of their acts—also on a simulated level. In simulation games, as in role playing, there is an opportunity for "reality practice" (albeit of a distinctly different kind than in role playing) in the sense that behavior can be tried out prior to the real-life performance and without the risks of real-life consequences.

One example of a fairly straightforward simulation game, and one which many teachers have probably already used without calling it by that name, is a game about supply and demand. Groups of students represent particular sectors of the commercial world chosen by either the teacher or the students, such as: truck-farmers → vegetable-canners → supermarkets → customers. These constitute the main elements in a production-and-sales system. Or one might choose another sector close to home, such as wholesalers, retailers, and customers in any industry which influences our daily lives directly—perhaps the food industry once again. Consumer strikes against the rise in meat prices are not yet ancient history and make a good producer-distributor-customer model. The basic model could also be applied to the production and sale of gasoline, clothing, or any other retail product. With slight changes, an equally simple model can be used to represent service-delivery systems, such as the postal service, or medical services.

To follow the rules of the game, let us say that all of the customers must purchase vital products, as in real life. The purchase of non-vital products remains optional. Wholesalers and retailers strive to sell their merchandise at the highest prices they can get on the market. At the start of the game, they set their prices as high as they can, and only as sales proceed will they find out if these prices are too high or too low, as determined by demand. By the end of the game, the students will have learned, in a relatively direct way, the law of supply-and-demand and its effect on prices at various levels in the economy. They will have learned these concepts even if they are not able to formulate them in so many words. The effects of this economic law will become apparent to the players when they use the resources represented (exchange of goods between wholesaler, retailer, and customer), and decide for themselves how to behave within the constraints of the system (how best to spend their money, the availability of specific products). By responding to the system in this way, they soon learn how the system responds to them. But remember: learning *how* a system functions is not the same as learning *about* the system, the latter usually being a much more verbal-didactic process. Students may need some help in putting their experience into words.

After participating in a game of this kind, a sixth-grade pupil, who amassed the largest profit as a retailer, was asked to tell the class what he had learned from playing the game. His first comment was "nothing, I just played." Then he was asked to describe some of his moves and actions in the game. There followed an illuminating description of how customers refused to buy from him because his prices were higher than his competitors'. He decided not to sell while others were conducting a price war. Soon they were all sold out and only he had any stock left, whereupon he raised his prices, making the most profit—as the customers had no alternative left but to buy from him. While all the factors leading to his commercial victory were obvious to this boy—indeed he had learned many important basic concepts—he was not comfortable using "official" terms such as the "law of supply-and-demand." It is questionable if he would rank high on an objective test of knowledge about the workings of our economic system. It seems equally unlikely that he would have acquired the knowledge he clearly possessed had the method of learning been an exclusively verbal one, as it usually is in our schools. Indeed, this example should raise doubts as to whether students who use abstract terminology freely really understand what this terminology expresses, without having had any *real* experience.

The reader should by now have a reasonably clear idea of what a simulation game can involve and how it functions. Before going into further detail we wish to point out the important place simulation games take in small-group teaching. Like role playing, they can form part of an integrated approach to classroom organization. They need not be used to achieve organizational, social, and/or motivational goals which are not otherwise achieved in the overall teaching effort. We believe that simulation games are most effective when they are used as an integral part of a teaching plan based on a social-systems view of the classroom in which students are learning cooperatively. The introduction of simulation games into the traditional classroom may serve some transient purposes, or may even act as a catalyst for change, but is not in itself likely to effect permanent change in the fundamental approach to teaching and learning.

Simulation games usually require small groups, although sometimes a large number of players can be involved. They explore social processes and skills through human interaction and problem-solving. Finally, they create conditions for learning through first-hand experience, making the learning vivid and relevant, rather than merely verbal and symbolic. Simulation games thus embody all the essential features of small-group learning and can be used effectively as one of its major techniques. The relevance of simulation games to small-group learning is substantially heightened when students take an active part in planning and designing the game, rather than importing ready-made products, although these too can be helpful. Doing research on the particular part of reality to be modeled, selecting its main features, creating the processes which represent the workings of the social system, deciding on the extent and use of available resources—these are all steps which make up an ideal context for stimulating small-group learning experiences, from both an intellectual and a social point of view (Boocock and Coleman, 1966; Boocock and Schild, 1968; Gordon, 1970; Nesbitt, 1971; Taylor and Walford, 1972).

Some Specific Qualities
of Simulation Games

Several qualities of simulation games deserve special mention, and discussion of these will also help clarify the nature of the games. The three outstanding features of simulation games we will discuss here are motivation, immediate evaluation of the results of experience, and the study of complex abstract processes through simplified representational behavior.

Motivation. Most descriptions of student participation in simulation games confirm that the players show great interest in the game, that games can arouse interest in the topic, and that they frequently contribute to more positive attitudes toward the topic. Players generally agree that the topic dealt with appears more interesting, more important, and more complicated than they had thought before the game (Cherryholmes, 1965; De Kock, 1969; Heinkel, 1970; Livingston and Stoll, 1973; Sharan and Colodner, 1975).

What are the characteristics of simulation games which make the players so enthusiastic about them? What is it about simulation games that heightens students' interest in the subject? (The following assumptions do not apply indiscriminately to *all* simulation games. Claims about potential effectiveness must be individually judged for each game on the basis of experience and observation. There are no doubt some simulation games whose effectiveness in accomplishing their declared goals is negligible.)

Unfortunately, the sparsity of research data does not provide us with definitive answers to these questions. (See the recent review by Livingston and Stoll, 1973.) What follows, therefore, are speculations based on a combination of our own experience and the available literature.

We surmise that the mutual support, interaction, and communication which motivate members of small groups in working together have a similar productive influence on participants in games. The pleasure a student derives from actively controlling his role and decisions instead of being a passive recipient of information (and of seeing almost immediately how his decisions affect those of his fellow students) is an important motivating force in simulation games. This does not necessarily imply that students will develop a greater sense of control over their environment as a result of participating in simulation games, as some authors have claimed. We contend merely that a sense of control is felt *during the game,* and that this feeling is of considerable motivational value.

The student's activity during the game has a dual character: performing his own task and influencing that of the other players. True, both activities are limited by the rules of the game and by the reactions of the other players. But these limits also define the individual's degrees of freedom: by telling him how far he *can* go, not only how far he may *not* go; therefore, they do not *limit* freedom in the true sense. Indeed, these limits are the basis of realism and relevance in the game; everyday life is bound by laws and social customs which are imperative for the survival of organized society. The important lesson for the student here is that he can observe and be aware of the consequences of his behavior and learn just what its scope and its limits are.

Even in light of the above, we would not expect that participation in simulation games would directly increase the student's capacity to control the real-life processes portrayed (Livingston and Stoll, 1973). We do, however, suggest that simulation games can go some way toward heightening his inner sense of control over his own decisions and environment. This is likely to develop when games are used as part of a general organization of the classroom into small groups, which, as we have already stressed, focuses on cooperation and equal participation. If students can take an active part in the planning and control of their learning environment, then both their self-confidence and their ability to take charge of the situation may possibly be improved. If this ability begins and ends with their participation in a game, it is not reasonable to expect them to develop a sense of greater control over real-life situations.

A second source of motivation is the simulation game's close resemblance to adult society. Educators claim that school prepares children for life in society, but few schools make much effort to explain to students the relevance of their studies to their adult lives and needs. If school studies are indeed meant to be a preparation for adult life, why is this not made clear? Too many students feel no personal involvement in school and the remote, purely "academic" pursuits it represents. Yet, study and research can, with the right approach, be made realistic and relevant.

Simulation games are taken directly from reality, and the "real-life" elements can be easily identified. Moreover, they often portray the adult society to which the student will soon belong. The games, therefore, can give the student a very real feeling of preparing for this society. The games encourage students to make responsible decisions in complex situations which they may well come across later in life, and this is usually not only a valuable experience but also a gratifying one for the students. The game must, of course, be within the students' scope and capabilities, otherwise it will be boring, meaningless, and even irritating. But a good simulation game allows for a very wide margin of behavior, adaptable to the ability of each participant, so that students will rarely feel that they are unable to cope. The "realistic" element is particularly marked in such a game, and this seems to be another

source of the high level of interest and involvement the participants feel. When playing a game with tenth and eleventh grade
students in a vocational high school, a colleague and one of the
authors found that the students were so absorbed in the *process*
that they were completely indifferent to the number of points to
be rewarded at the end (Sharan and Colodner, 1975).

We wish to point out that realism and relevance are not to be
identified solely with the contemporary and the concrete. Simulation games are not an ideal medium for studying, say, extended
historical processes, but they can be a powerful way of representing historical events. Very abstract, cultural, or intellectual
issues may also be clarified through the game experience. Games
are not limited to representing our immediate world, although that
too is amazingly complex and merits much investigation.

Immediate evaluation. One of the important features of
simulation games is the feedback mechanism in the game process,
which provides almost immediate information about the consequences of behavior and the chance to modify it in light of this
knowledge. Players can see the effects of their decisions on the
game's progress and, if necessary, alter their decisions accordingly.
Despite awareness of the importance of feedback in processing
information, many forms of education still allow considerable
time lapse between the completion of learning tasks and the
receipt of some evaluation of the student's performance, with the
frequent result that the student no longer makes the effort to
correct or improve his performance. In this case, evaluation is not
feedback, which should be defined here as adjusting the *process* on
the basis of knowledge of the *results*. Even more negative is
evaluation which is purely quantitative, merely indicating the
number of right or wrong answers. Qualitative evaluations are less
common, but it is these which explain mistakes and help the
students improve their approach to problems. In simulation games,
however, players learn quickly and naturally about the results of
their decisions, without feeling that they are being judged. They

simply see for themselves whether their decisions have produced the desired results. Furthermore, this type of evaluation is a part of their general activity, not some form imposed on them—such as a grade—and therefore unrelated to the process itself. It resembles real-life feedback mechanisms, since *results* are usually our source of knowledge about our activities; in adult society there are no good marks from the teacher. The student's information about his results in the game comes also from his peers, rather than solely from the teacher—a much more realistic situation.

Clearly, therefore, games should provide the players with evaluations or some other technique whereby they can assess the applicability of their decisions, according to unambiguous criteria. (Setting up criteria for evaluation is discussed in greater detail later in this chapter.)

In the traditional classroom, the pupil knows that the right answer to any question will emerge if he just waits long enough. If the teacher doesn't give the answer, then some other student will produce it. Simulation games are a much less cut-and-dried system, in which the correct answers are not really known in advance either to the teacher or to any student in the class. Participation in such an experience is in itself a novelty and a challenge for students. The "best solution" is hidden in the future—no one knows exactly how to reach it nor is anyone certain what it really is. This brings a dramatic dimension to simulation games and stimulates the players to take a creative-experimental approach. The flexibility and openness of the game give the students a greater degree of freedom than when they are required to find a single acceptable answer. They can act according to guess or judgment, and may use their imaginative ability as well as logic in directing their progress in the game.

Since the information necessary to an evaluation of student performance is acquired from the game itself, teachers are relieved of the role of judge and dispenser of grades. Conversely, the students are also spared the unpleasantness of being perpetually evaluated by the teacher. The type of evaluation we advocate is more objective from both these points of view (Gordon, 1970).

Studying complex processes. One of the major teaching goals of simulation games is to create suitable conditions for students to become personally involved in formulating hypotheses, and in planning and carrying out experiments by which to examine complex social processes, whether political, commercial, historical, military, or familial. Players should be able to deepen their appreciation for the complexity of the social system represented in the game, clarifying it and having greater understanding of its interrelated elements than they did beforehand. Or, at least, any understanding already acquired through more traditional methods should be considerably enhanced by more direct participation in the workings of the system (Lewis and Wentworth, 1971).

In a game exploring the pollution problem, students can represent various points of view in both the public and private sectors, such as economic, political, technological, and social interests. Each player (or group of players) must consider other points of view in order to work out his own attitude to all involved parties. All parties negotiate throughout the game for their particular interests as representatives of themselves, other people, institutions, municipal and/or federal governments, industry, citizens groups, or professional organizations. The conflict between the various viewpoints will emerge in the arguments aired during the negotiations.

A game about pollution could be the culmination of an extensive research project, with the planning and actual process of playing the game serving as key techniques for some or all of the groups to present the result of their research to their classmates. Instead of merely assembling the students in order for each group to present a verbal summary of its findings (in other words, conducting a series of separate lectures), and running the familiar risk of boredom, it would be a good idea for groups to summarize their work in various original ways, one being a simulation game.

From it, players will learn what the main sources of pollution are; who is most affected by it and how; where the social power concerning pollution really lies; what means are available to overcome it and at what cost; what the political and economic forces are doing to combat—or ignore—pollution; the difficulties of arriving at a compromise suitable to all parties; and the short- and long-term consequences of any delay in eliminating, or at least checking, pollution. A simulation game covering all of these issues can be planned and carried out by the students, with the help of their teacher, as part of a broader project. A game of this type can be undertaken even by fourth or fifth grade students, if informational resources appropriate to their level of comprehension can be found. Of course, students should not merely outline the causes of the problem, but go on to seek solutions.

These thumbnail descriptions of possible games indicate the many levels on which knowledge can be acquired in a simulation game. These levels can include: information; skills; feelings; concepts; understanding of others' motives; understanding of relationships between the parties; and understanding the relationship of the game's model (micro-reality) to the real world (macro-reality). These levels may also be viewed as indicators of the player's expanding scope of awareness which becomes more encompassing as the game progresses. The broader the scope of the students' understanding, the more they understand their relationships to each other and the more integrated their game is likely to become.

Productive participation in a game may be unrelated to students' verbal ability. Games have interactive and strategic components which do not demand expressive talents, and are therefore a valuable teaching method for students who are not verbally gifted (Abt, 1971; Lewis and Wentworth, 1971).

The Virtues of Planning
Your Own Games

There is an already substantial and continually growing list of simulation games available commercially. (See inventories available in Livingston and Stoll, 1973; Taylor and Walford, 1972; Twelker, 1970; Zuckerman and Horn, 1973.) It is important to participate in a good game which has been tried and tested. Alongside the use of prepared games, many of which are relatively complex, we urge teachers to work with students on planning and playing original games designed to suit the particular needs of the class. Students can find the investment of their time and energy in research, design, and playing their own games more rewarding and instructive than using ready-made ones. Without intending to detract at all from the benefit of existing games, we nevertheless wish to emphasize that simulation games are one technique in the context of small-group teaching in which student planning and participation in learning tasks are of paramount importance. Total dependence on commercial games is not desirable because it takes the initiative and personal responsibility away from the teacher and students and reverts to ready-made materials for "teacher-proof" and "student-proof" classrooms. While claiming to encourage involvement and individual decision-making, games can still foster the same dependence as so many other "prepackaged goods" in the curriculum.

Social scientists who have contributed so much to the development of simulation games have always been careful to make public the principles behind their work, and, at the same time as preparing games for commercial distribution, have encouraged teachers to create their own games. In this light we will review the principles currently available for the design and construction of simulation games.

A good simulation game does not have to be very complicated. Teachers and students can plan and play games which are relatively short (a half hour) and straightforward, but still provide very memorable experiences. The game's complexity is not a measure of its effectiveness.

Preparing a game can be very time-consuming. Not all the

work need be done in class. Indeed, this is an excellent opportunity for creative and cooperative homework. The class can divide up into groups to do their homework projects, each group dealing with a different part of the game. It is important for all groups to understand the general plan of the game and how their contribution will fit into the whole unit.

Role Playing and Simulation Games

Before reviewing steps for designing simulation games, some comments are needed to further distinguish role playing from simulation games in order to sharpen our grasp of the game.

One object of role playing is spontaneous portrayal of natural behavior in social situations, and the development of the players' and observers' understanding of the role. The object of simulation games, however, is to cultivate understanding of how the role can or must function within the system, i.e., how a person or group works because of the legal, military, social, economic, or institutional constraints involved. This understanding need not include empathy for the person's feelings or thoughts, though this might help the player to calculate his moves in the game. Playing the role of oneself, another individual, or a group in the affective sense can indeed be part of a simulation game, but is not a requisite part. The interactions here are governed by the laws or modes of operation actually existing in the system under investigation. Therefore, in order for the players to achieve their goals, all parts of the game must fit together just as they do in reality. In role playing, on the other hand, the *affective* and *social* encounter is of paramount importance, and there are no rules governing this encounter other than the reasonable approximation of behavior in these circumstances. Moreover, the portrayal of human interaction in itself is sufficient as a goal in role playing. Taking all these points into consideration, it is clear that the planning and performing of role playing differs vastly from the planning and performing of simulation games. This in no way reduces the importance and effectiveness of role playing as an educational technique. We do not share the view that role playing is a "poor man's simulation game." They are separate, sometimes complementary, techniques, and their goals and potential achievements are *not* interchangeable.

Designing a Simulation Game

The planning of a simulation game should proceed in stages. After all the critical questions have been answered once, the planners may wish to review them and change whatever they consider necessary to make a better integrated unit. Gordon (1970) has suggested that planners should make a series of work sheets listing all the main problems on one side and all the tentative solutions on the other. On each subsequent work sheet in the series, new formulations and changes will be listed. The series ends when the plans are considered satisfactory, at least until the game goes through a trial run.

Below is a sample work sheet which poses some typical questions with which planners might be faced. Not all the questions may be relevant to every game. (These same questions appear in more elaborate form in the discussion of the stages in the design of simulation games which appears following the work sheet.)

Work Sheet*

Typical questions to be answered

1. Objectives
   a. list your educational objectives
   b. translate educational objectives into behavioral ones

1.
   a. What do you want the participants to learn? Skills, information, feelings, concepts, system constraints, system process?
   b. What kind of behavior should participants perform in order to demonstrate that they achieved the educational objective?

*The authors are indebted to Bonnie Belkin for her valuable contributions to the formulation of this work sheet.

2. Real-life situation

3. General model of the game
   determine the roles needed
4. Interactions
   a. determine the game structure

   b. determine the game's procedures

   c. consider the kind of learning desired when determining 4a and 4b

5. Resources
   a. determine the media of inter-action

2. What is the most specific description you can give of the situation to be modeled?

3. What roles, if any, are to be represented? (Some games have none.) Are the roles to be individuals, groups, institutions, nations?

4.
   a. Who deals with whom? Can everyone interact with everyone else? If not, what are the restrictions?

   b. In what way are the parties to interact? Do they buy and sell, fight, debate, cooperate, compete? What exactly are they to do with each other?

   c. Does the game intend to teach information, skills, feelings, processes? If information, then some type of classifying scheme should be included, or the teaching of a skill for using the information. If a concept is to be learned, then the game should allow for the application of the concept in different situations. If the game emphasizes feelings, then getting points for satisfaction or frustration should be emphasized. If skills are important, opportunities for practice will be needed.

5.
   a. What means or sources of power are appropriate for the roles through which the participants can express themselves and conduct their affairs? Are the resources money, shares, votes, troops, knowledge, etc.?

b. determine the quantity of resources

b. How much of these resources is to be allocated to each role at the start of the game? Have you considered the inequalities found in reality when determining the allocation?

6. Schedule of events
determine a sequence for performing the game's activities

6. In what order do players make their moves? Is the sequence of moves clear to all participants? How is the game to start? Who makes the first move and what will this be?

7. Rules
determine the rules governing the interaction in the game

7.

a. What laws or other limitations govern the real-life situation represented in the game?

b. How can the laws affecting the real-life system be translated into rules of the game?

c. Are there any specific acts which players may not perform?

d. Are the rules simple and few in number so they can be easily learned and observed and not inhibit the game's progress?

8. Scoring Criteria
a. determine how a team or individual can win

8.

a. Does the game have an internal winner, such as: the most satisfied person, the first to reach a given goal, the one who gets his way, the nation which conquers the most territory, the candidate who gets the most votes? Are the criteria for winning clearly related to the players' resources?

b. determine the way players learn of their success or failure

b. Do players receive information about their position during each round, at the end of each round, or only once at the end of the game? How will the timing of this information affect their conduct in the game?

9. Materials

9. What equipment is needed to facilitate the functioning of the game's processes? Does the game require a playing board, role profiles, a scenario, a data bank, score cards, information cards, dice, spinners, special signs, toys?

You are now ready to write out all the details of your game.

10. Write and design the materials and game components listed above

10.

   a. Write an outline of the scenario (if one is included in the materials).

   b. Write role profiles. Prepare one index card for each profile, and list on the card where each player is located and what he does in each stage of the game. Group cards according to their first appearance in the game sequence. On separate sheets of paper list all the ideas you want to transmit, to be discussed or to be investigated during the game. Divide these ideas among the role profiles, keeping in mind when the players will be exchanging ideas during the game.

   c. Expand each role profile to more life-like proportions. For example, you might include information about family background, economic background, character, feelings, attitudes, strivings and goals, friends, enemies, affiliations.

11. Write instructions for the game leader and participants

11. The instructions should include a description of the materials included in the game, its objectives, the roles for participating, and procedures for playing the game. Also, directions

should be offered on how to use the game with different numbers of players, the physical facilities required, and how to lengthen or shorten the game according to the level of the students. Suggestions should be made to the game leader as to how he can ensure that the game proceeds smoothly.

Write instructions for players, if necessary. Include the game's objectives, preparations for the game, procedures, and any special rules.

12. Test the game and rewrite items as necessary

Choosing a topic and setting goals. One of the major uses of simulation games is the exploration of processes in which a number of parties are involved in relationships or negotiations of some sort. Games are not intended for teaching facts alone or simple descriptive materials which can be learned and fully understood by reading. They are meant to give students experience of ideas which might otherwise remain purely abstract.

The first question to be answered at the design stage is: What do we want to learn? What are our goals? Is our objective to acquire a particular *concept*, such as "balance of forces" (in international, East-West relations, either political or military, or within an institution, such as a hospital, factory, or city hall); supply and demand; battle of the sexes; status and power? Or perhaps we might prefer to investigate a process, such as: a workers' strike, pollution, urban transportation, school desegregation, or electing a mayor. Or, on still another plane, perhaps students might wish to simulate a society or culture in which behavior is based on customs and laws differing sharply from our own: fishing in the Trobriand Islands, or setting up a work schedule in a kibbutz. After a topic has been selected and defined, specific aims must be formulated to guide the design of the game; otherwise, it will be difficult to decide which elements from the real-life situation should be included in the game.

Let us examine the suggestions above. Some are clear and specific, others are general, even vague. The topics suggested in the form of concepts are mostly vague, and really only propose an idea as a starting point for discussion. Within each of these are many possibilities for more specific topics. "A workers' strike" is a much more specific subject, as are "school desegregation," and "electing a mayor." However, even these must be narrowed down through discussion before the design stage can begin. If we wish to learn the meaning of the concept "a workers' strike," we may want to include different strikes under different conditions. Or, do we want to represent in the game the dynamic aspects of any strike, showing the relationship between labor and management, workers and union leaders, and the negotiation process?

Building a model of relationships. What is the precise situation to be represented in the game and who is involved in it? The answers to these questions provide the basis for the model of the game. How these figures interact and what they do to or with each other determines the nature of the players' relationships. Together, these decisions form the basic structure of the game. Typical roles are public or professional figures: political leaders, union leaders, government officials such as the Secretary of Defense or the Secretary of State, executives, industrialists, airline pilots, businessmen, engineers, and so on. Not *all* the roles or parties involved must appear in the game; it is possible to overload a game with too many roles, thus detracting attention from the main issue. Furthermore, the aim is to explore a specific reality by representing a critical part of it, not to reproduce that reality in all of its manifestations. The roles or parties to be chosen must exert a decisive influence on the functioning of the real-life situation. All other figures should be excluded, or represented in name only, by a passing reference or by some mechanical means (a sign, drawing).

The position of the various parties in the situation must be spelled out, as well as the means at their disposal for reaching their goals. How do they use these resources to express their relationships to the other parties? What exactly do they wish to achieve? In other words, by what means do the parties communicate; how is their relative power assessed; and what do they want to do with this power? The resources available and the way they are used should bear some relation—direct or symbolic—to real life. They can be very simple, or relatively complex. These resources and the rules governing their use have great influence on the players' behavior.

The only thing in a simulation game resembling a script is a schedule of events setting out some sequence of acts. Players must know if some moves have to come first, or if everyone is free to act whenever he considers it reasonable to do so. It is helpful to state clearly how the game is to begin and end; otherwise, players may waste time wondering how to start.

Choosing roles and players. How many players should participate in a simulation game? The answer is clear: as many as can be actively involved all the time. "Active involvement" means that no one sits on the sidelines watching. Several sets of players can carry on parallel activities; or the class can be divided into two sections, each playing a separate game; or roles can be taken by groups of players instead of only one.

With careful division into small groups, the absolute number of participants may not be an important issue at all. Organizational considerations of the game are much more important.

Resources and goals. Alongside the game model which identifies the players and explains their relationships, there must be resources which players need in order to perform. These can take on a variety of forms, including abstract ones such as information (sometimes the only resource in a game); or feelings; or some form of property, people, votes, or rights. These resources are often represented symbolically by tokens, paper money, documents, drawings, or toys. They are exchanged among players in an effort to influence the progress of the game and to reach its goals. It is often the amount of resources accumulated by various players which decides the winners and losers, although this need not be the case. They can also be determined by the accuracy of the information they give or some criterion other than mere quantity. But it is advisable to agree on criteria for evaluating more or less successful performance.

The basic model of the game should help in deciding what quantity of resources each player should receive at the start. Obviously, industrialists have more resources than employees, or landlords more than tenants. Status order in real life must be truly reflected. It is sometimes possible to distribute certain resources equally (such as information), where the game is based on competition between players in the effective use of the resource. Equal distribution makes scoring at the end of the game easier. The amount of resources to be allocated to various parties is sometimes decided only after several trial runs. If one group wins easily all the time, it might be that their share of resources gives them unfair advantages over others. One player may feel no pressure to negotiate because his resources are in no danger of being depleted. Such a situation would obviously weaken the game.

The nature and quantity of resources also influence the goals for which the players strive. Indeed, resources should be determined by the game's designers in light of the players' goals. Goals are also an important factor in each player's position. All the information about the orientation, goals, and resources of a role can be presented to players in the form of a role profile, which gives a background on which each player can base his behavior. This background material should include some information about his goals in relation to the other roles in the game. Does he intend to acquire a fortune, change his living conditions, achieve a peace treaty with another country, or improve the neighborhood?

The goals stated in these profiles should not be so rigid that the players cannot alter them according to the progress of the game. No reasonable moves should be eliminated in advance unless they are quite incompatible with the role. If a player sees that a different technique will help him achieve his goal, then he should be free to try it. His own best interests are a good guide for planning his behavior. In short, the profile should provide basic suggestions for appropriate behavior, but should not commit the player irrevocably to any one set of actions.

Formulating rules for decision-making. The decisions made by the players are the essence of the game. In a game called "Courtroom," the lawyer's decision about which questions to ask a witness will determine the progress of the case, as in real life. When a lawyer cross-examines a witness, there are certain types of questions, or certain formulations of them, which he may not use. Any such prohibitions must appear in the rules of a simulation game about a trial. In preparation for the game, students might interview a lawyer, attend an actual trial and, of course, read relevant material. The subject of the trial in the "Courtroom" game should be relevant to the students' lives or to a broader subject which they are already studying.

The formulation of the game's rules will clearly depend upon the information available about the real-life situation. In a military game, the scene of the battle must be decided upon, as must the number of troops involved at any given point, and the strength of the enemy's forces must be estimated. These decisions will be based on the information possessed by the Commanding Officer and his staff. It may be a part of the rules that only general staff may make this kind of decision. In a game called "Contractor," about the building industry, decisions about the price of a building must take into consideration the cost of the land, materials, labor costs, and so on. The game may involve competition between contractors for building contracts from the city government, in which case some rules about permissible means of competition will have to be established, Should contractors be allowed to cut labor costs by paying minority laborers less than the minimum wage? The game should recreate real-life competition so that students utilize the available information to help them toward the desired goal, such as increasing profits.

Too many restricting rules stifle the game. Not *all* the laws pertaining to the real-life situation need appear in the game. The choice of rules and procedures should be as selective as that of the parties represented; in fact, a good simulation game will be bound by as few rules as possible. However, the rules and prohibitions must always be in keeping with the real-life situation. For example, if the subject under study is non-violent resistance, the students may want to design a game about Mohandas Gandhi's struggle against the British in India. If so, Gandhi's followers must display no physical resistance (symbolic, of course) to any acts of the British.

Schedule of events. It is helpful to provide some kind of background schedule to guide players through the game. There should be some pointer toward how and when to start and finish the game. This does not mean that all moves are predetermined, only that certain moves must come before others. In some games, dice or spinners are used to determine, on a chance basis, who moves first. In others, the sequence is simply a series of steps which follow each other logically, such as in "Counselor" (Sharan and Colodner, 1975), where the class divides into groups of four, each group member reading the first role profile; all groups then discuss the information given in the profile and relate it to the occupations which might be appropriate for this "client," according to the classification system appearing on the playing board. The discussion constitutes part of the game's "action" and is not determined by any sequence of events.

A planned action sequence also prevents undesirable discontinuities and delays. The sequence might establish specific time spans for each round in the game and for the game as a whole, depending on the situation. However, if time limits are not an element of the real-life situation, they should not be imposed on the game either.

Criteria for evaluation. The criteria for winning or losing the game must be based on the goals being aimed at. The winner is usually the party who increases his resources to the greatest extent. Determining these criteria can be more difficult if the game is based on a social topic which may not have clear quantitative outcomes. But most achievements can be translated into quantitative terms: who achieved more court decisions in his favor, who achieved better conditions for prison inmates, who established more military bases in the Far or Middle East, who was able to offer his client more accurate advice, and so on. All of these can be linked to a point system to help measure success. The game's objectives can also be listed on a scale of priorities, awarding more points for achieving the more important objectives. Furthermore, students will understand the game better, perhaps even improve upon it, if they have to analyze it and measure their success in points. Setting up evaluation criteria is an essential part of the learning experience associated with the planning and playing of simulation games.

Some simulation games involve students so totally and are so intrinsically interesting that the final scores may be of only minor interest. In others, it may be difficult to evaluate performance without a scoring system, in which case students will not really understand their part in the game. A well-defined scoring system can clarify the goals of the game and thereby help players direct their activities. Players should be able to see clearly that their success or failure in a game is not a measure of their *ability* to cope with learning materials in general, but rather a reflection of their use of strategy in that particular game. The results of the game will explain how and where they made mistakes, and provide them with valuable experience, according to which they will correct their moves next time.

Observations About Simulation Gaming

If teachers understand the workings of simulation games, they will be able to help students use them efficiently, even if they are purchased commercially. Not all of the features listed above must or do appear in every game. The issues discussed here are no more than a set of guidelines which can be helpful in planning games. However, game construction is not an exact science; it requires imagination, initiative, hard work, and revision based on trial and error. There is also no substitute for a clear analysis of the reality to be represented and good judgment in the selection of parties and situations to be simulated. We are certain that once teachers and students have had a successful experience with a simulation game, they will be eager to use such games more often.

Like many other experiences with a social-emotional dimension, the best way to learn about them is to try them out. It is not advisable to begin with a long introduction about the theory of simulation games, or with a list of the do's and don'ts of the game, before students have actually participated in a good game. We recommend a practical approach, with experience serving as a basis for logical analysis afterwards. When using a ready-made game for the first game experience, encourage players to volunteer quickly and play without much delay. The first run is really a trial, and may have to be repeated before players grasp all of the game's implications. In any case, the game should get under way with minimum preparation. During the debriefing session, which is usually indispensable, the game's concepts, aims, and methods can be discussed.

A debriefing session after the game should touch upon the following questions: (1) What did the players experience as they progressed? (2) How do they understand the relationship between the game and the reality on which it is based? (3) What principles, concepts, or experiences did the game teach? This discussion could be a basis for a replay if this would be considered instructive, but replays are not necessarily productive, and should not be undertaken as a matter of course. Only if a replay is definitely considered worthwhile should it be tried. It is possible, however, that the players may wish to try a new approach which occurred to them only after playing the game once. They may have grasped some new point which leads to a fresh outlook or to introducing new elements into the game.

A Simulation Game: "Negotiations"

Following are elements from which it is possible to construct a simulation game about some form of negotiations between rival groups. We have posed a series of questions which a game designer might wish to answer, or to use as a prototype for additional questions. This general format can be used with a variety of content, so the particular parties to the negotiations and the specific problems they are to solve must be determined by the designer of the game. Completing this game can be viewed as an exercise in game construction.

Objectives. What should the game teach?
1. Skills (how to conduct negotiations, formal discussions, etc.).
2. Concepts (different types of negotiation, labor-management disputes, international conflicts, scientific debates relating to the arms race, etc.).
3. Understanding conflicting viewpoints.
4. Understanding the complex nature of international relations.
5. Learning about specific political or intergroup conflicts.

Roles. There are many different kinds of negotiations, each requiring a different approach, such as military, international negotiations at summit level, international negotiations regarding economic affairs (such as the Common Market), disarmament talks, negotiations between union officials and management of industry, community groups and officials of city hall, etc.

Resources and materials. Resources can be information

provided to representatives, such as policy statements, military data, information about resources needed for economic agreements, and territorial issues. Representatives must have adequate knowledge of the particular topics in order to engage intelligently in the negotiations.

Materials needed for the game might be: identification tags for representatives, stating name and position or country, name plates to be placed on the table during the negotiations, formats of documents to be exchanged or agreements to be signed, and the appropriate arrangement of the "conference hall."

Schedule of events. A series of meetings for negotiations can conveniently be divided into sessions corresponding to the rounds of the game, and these can be of limited time span if necessary. Also, different kinds of sessions can be scheduled in advance, to ensure steady progress. Thus, a program could follow an outline like this:

1. Preparatory meetings of individual delegations (1 hour).
2. Opening session. Speeches by primary representatives of each delegation (1 hour).
3. Negotiating session (half hour).
4. General session to review progress at all levels (half hour).
5. Second negotiating session (half hour).
6. Session to formulate specific terms of agreement (half hour).
7. Final session for signing agreements (half hour).

Rules and interactions.

1. Who may negotiate with whom?
2. What kinds of transactions are prohibited?
3. How many speakers may participate in the general session?
4. How many representatives is each party permitted to send to the conference?
5. What agreements must be reached?

Evaluation. Each nation's (or party's) objectives should be listed in order of priority and scored appropriately. They must, however, be kept secret and not revealed to their rivals. Priorities must therefore be determined during the pre-conference meeting of each delegation, and copies of them deposited with some neutral party. This list will be used later to score each group's achievements in the negotiations.

* * *

It is possible to purchase simulation games and to provide students with interesting and instructive experiences without their having participated in preparatory research or in planning the game. However, the above outline of negotiation games illustrates how simulations can be integrated into a broad program of small-group learning which includes most, if not all, the techniques discussed in this book. With the proper guidance from the teacher, students can plan and carry out an entire sequence of studies, from the initial investigation of a topic through the planning and playing of a simulation game, incorporating the main features of the topic being studied. This approach to teaching can provide students with a large measure of self-direction in determining the nature of their work in school, with a sense of relevance regarding the content of their studies, and with the opportunity to be actively involved in the pursuit of knowledge in cooperation with their peers.

Postscript to Teaching Staffs

If you or your colleagues do not feel fully competent in the application of small-group techniques in the classroom, or if you wish to improve your skills, we recommend that these skills be practiced on the staff itself. Teachers can replace student groups. The techniques described here, such as cooperative planning, allocation of roles to different group members, buzz groups, systematic observation of discussion skills, and so on, can be practiced by subdividing the staff into small groups and conducting a group exercise. Groups of teachers might simulate classroom conditions, or, more realistically, work on actual problems confronting themselves. They could even work on the problem of how to improve their own teaching techniques!

One approach is to have small groups of teachers (four to six or seven persons) study and practice various small-group teaching techniques for presentation to the rest of the staff. The aim of each group will be to plan and direct the experiences which teachers need most in order to acquire the fundamental skills of a given technique. Thus, for example, one group could be responsible for learning centers. In order to instruct colleagues in the construction and uses of these centers, the group could use slides, placards displaying theoretical principles, and, most important, prepare an exhibition of learning centers incorporating features which need to be demonstrated. The teachers will then attend this exhibition, work at the various centers, and experience for themselves the way in which the learning centers can best be utilized. Similar suggestions can be applied to all small-group techniques.

Role playing and simulations in particular are highly recommended for use by groups of teachers to explore problems in the classroom or in staff relations or to improve teaching skills. In effect we are recommending that role playing and simulations be used by the teaching staff in a manner similar to that suggested for the students, namely, *as a means of facilitating the use of other small-group techniques*, as a form of practice-teaching, and as a means of encouraging constructive comments from colleagues. One may certainly expect that teachers who have an opportunity to practice these teaching methods *outside* the classroom are likely to use them with greater confidence and skill *inside* the classroom.

If small groups of teachers can meet to further their own professional development, they give themselves an excellent opportunity for experimentation and practical testing of new teaching techniques. They can conduct their own in-service training workshops through mutual cooperation in small groups (Rubin, 1971). Some schools might have to seek the help of an outside consultant, perhaps someone trained in organization development, to ensure the success of these workshops in renewing the staff's outlook and skills (Schmuck and Miles, 1971). Other schools may already have a tradition of mutual assistance as among teachers of grade-units or similar subject-matter areas. These sub-units are often an ideal framework for investigating and trying out new approaches to classroom teaching, and for finding solutions to problems which confront teachers each day of their professional lives.

References

Abt, C. Games for Learning. In S. Boocock and E. Schild (Eds.) *Simulation Games in Learning.* Beverly Hills, California: Sage Publications, 1968, 65-84.

Abt, C. *Serious Games.* New York: The Viking Press, 1971.

Anderson, R. and Kell, B. Student attitudes about participation in classroom groups. *Journal of Educational Research*, 1954, *48*, 255-267.

Argyle, M. *The Psychology of Interpersonal Behavior.* Baltimore, Maryland: Penguin Books, 1967.

Argyle, M. and Dean, J. Eye-contact, distance, and affiliation. *Sociometry*, 1965, *28*, 289-304.

Baker, J., Ross, J., and Walters, B. *Each One Learning: A Small Group Process Manual for Teachers.* San Bernardino, California: Regional Project Office, San Bernardino County Schools, 1971.

Baker, J., Smith, T., Walters, B. and Wetzel, R. *They Help Each Other Learn.* San Bernardino, California: San Bernardino County Schools, 1971.

Bany, M. and Johnson, L. *Classroom Group Behavior.* New York: Macmillan Co., 1964.

Barth, R. *Open Education and the American School.* New York: Agathon Press, 1973.

Benne, K.D., Bradford, L.P., and Lippitt, R. Stages in the process of group thinking and discussion. In K.D. Benne (Ed.),

Human Relations in Curriculum Change. New York: Dryden Press, 1951, 68-84.

Bennis, W. and Shepard, H. A theory of group development. *Human Relations,* 1956, *9,* 415-437.

Berkowitz, L. Group standards, cohesiveness, and productivity. *Human Relations,* 1954, *7,* 505-519.

Bishop, L. *Individualizing Educational Systems.* New York: Harper and Row, 1971.

Blackhurst, A. Sociodrama for the adolescent mentally retarded. *Training School Bulletin,* 1966, *63,* 136-142.

Blackie, J. *Inside the Primary School.* New York: Schocken Publishing Company, 1971.

Blitz, B. *The Open Classroom: Making It Work.* Boston, Massachusetts: Allyn and Bacon, 1973.

Bloom, B. *et al.* (Eds.) *Taxonomy of Educational Objectives Handbook I: Cognitive Domain.* New York: David McKay, 1956.

Boocock, S. From luxury item to learning tool. In S. Boocock and E. Schild (Eds.), *Simulation Games in Learning.* Beverly Hills, California: Sage Publications, 1968, 53-64.

Boocock, S. and Coleman, J. Games with simulated environments in learning. *Sociology of Education,* 1966, *39,* 215-236.

Boocock, S. and Schild, E. (Eds.) *Simulation Games in Learning.* Beverly Hills, California: Sage Publications, 1968.

Bormann, E. *Discussion and Group Methods.* New York: Harper and Row, 1969.

Bovard, E. Interaction and attraction to the group. *Human Relations,* 1956, *9,* 481-489.

Brilhart, J. *Effective Group Discussion.* Dubuque, Iowa: William C. Brown Co., 1967.

Burton, W. *The Guidance of Learning Activities* (3rd Ed.). New York: Appleton-Century-Crofts, 1962.

Cartwright, D. and Zander, A. *Group Dynamics: Research and Theory.* New York: Harper and Row, 1968.

Cherryholmes, C. Developments in simulation of international relations in high-school teaching. *Phi Delta Kappan*, 1965, *46*, 227-231.

Chesler, M. and Fox, R. *Role-Playing Methods in the Classroom*. Chicago: Science Research Associates, 1966.

Cogan, M. The behavior of teachers and the productive behavior of their pupils. *Journal of Experimental Education*, 1958, *27*, 89-105.

Cohen, E. Modifying the effects of social structure. *American Behavioral Scientist*, 1973, *16*, 861-878.

Cohen, E. and Roper, S. Modification of interracial interaction disability. *American Sociological Review*, 1972, *37*, 643-657.

Collins, B. and Guetzkow, H. *A Social Psychology of Group Processes for Decision Making*. New York: John Wiley and Sons, 1964.

Collins, B. and Raven, B. Group structure: Attraction, coalitions, communication and power. In G. Lindzey and E. Aronson (Eds.), *The Handbook of Social Psychology* (Vol. 4; 2nd edition). Reading, Massachusetts: Addison-Wesley, 1969, 102-204.

Corsini, R. *Roleplaying in Psychotherapy: A Manual*. Chicago: Aldine Publishing Company, 1966.

Cote, B. and Gurske, B. *Learning Center Guides*. San Jose, California: CTM, 1970.

Cratty, B. *Active Learning: Games to Enhance Academic Abilities*. Englewood Cliffs, New Jersey: Prentice Hall, 1971.

Davis, J. *Group Performance*. Reading, Massachusetts: Addison-Wesley, 1969.

Dawe, H. The influence of the size of kindergarten group upon performance. *Child Development*, 1934, *5*, 295-303.

De Charms, R. *Personal Causation*. New York: Academic Press, 1968.

De Charms, R. From pawns to origins: Toward self motivation. In G. Lesser (Ed.), *Psychology and Educational Practice*.

Glenview, Illinois: Scott, Foresman and Co., 1971, 380-470.

De Kock, P. Simulations and changes in racial attitudes. *Social Education*, February 1969, 181-183.

Deutsch, M. The effects of cooperation and competition upon group process. In D. Cartwright and A. Zander (Eds.), *Group Dynamics*. New York: Harper and Row, 1968, 461-482.

Dunkin, M. and Biddle, B. *The Study of Teaching*. New York: Holt, Rinehart, and Winston, Inc., 1974.

Elms, A. *Role Playing, Reward, and Attitude Change*. New York: Van Nostrand Reinhold, 1969.

Feffer, M. The cognitive implications of role-taking behavior. *Journal of Personality*, 1959, *27*, 152-168.

Feffer, M. and Gourevitch, V. Cognitive aspects of role-taking in children. *Journal of Personality*, 1966, *28*, 383-396.

Fiedler, F. *A Theory of Leadership Effectiveness*. New York: McGraw-Hill, 1967.

Flanders, N. *Teaching with Groups*. Minneapolis, Minnesota: Burgess Publishing Co., 1954.

Flavell, J. *The Development of Role-Taking and Communication Skills in Children*. New York: John Wiley and Sons, 1968.

Gardner, D. *Experiment and Tradition in Primary Schools*. London: Methuen and Co., 1966.

Gerard, H. Some effects of status, role clarity, and group goal clarity upon the individual's relations to group processes. *Journal of Personality*, 1957, *27*, 477-488.

Gibb, C. The principles and traits of leadership. *Journal of Abnormal and Social Psychology*, 1947, *42*, 267-284.

Gibb, C. Leadership. In G. Lindzey and E. Aronson (Eds.), *The Handbook of Social Psychology* (Vol. 4; 2nd edition). Reading, Massachusetts: Addison-Wesley, 1969, 205-282.

Gibb, J. The effects of group size and of threat reduction upon creativity in a problem solving situation. *American Psychologist*, 1951, *6*, 324.

Glasser, J. *The Elementary School Learning Center for Indepen-*

dent Study. West Nyack, New York: Parker Publishing Co., 1971.

Glidewell, J. *et al*. Socialization and social structure in the classroom. In M. Hoffman and L. Hoffman (Eds.), *Review of Child Development Research*. New York: Russell Sage Foundation, 1966, 221-256.

Gordon, A. *Games for Growth*. Palo Alto, California: Science Research Associates, 1970.

Gordon, T. *Group Centered Leadership*. Boston, Massachusetts: Houghton-Mifflin, 1955.

Gorman, A. *Teachers and Learners: The Interactive Process of Education*. Boston, Massachusetts: Allyn and Bacon, 1969.

Graham, C. Sociodrama as a teaching technique. *Social Studies*, 1960, *51*, 257-259.

Greenberg, M. Role-playing to motivate acceptable behavior. *Health Education Journal*, 1961, *24*, 6-7.

Gulley, H. *Discussion, Conference, and Group Process* (2nd Ed.). New York: Holt, Rinehart, and Winston, 1968.

Haas, R. (Ed.) *Psychodrama and Sociodrama in American Education*. New York: Beacon House, 1949.

Haigh, G. and Schmidt, W. The learning of subject matter in teacher centered and group centered classes. *Journal of Educational Psychology*, 1956, *47*, 295-301.

Hanna, L., Potter, G., and Hageman, N. *Unit Teaching in the Elementary School*. New York: Holt, Rinehart, and Winston, 1961.

Hare, A. A study of interaction and consensus in different sized groups. *American Sociological Review*, 1952, *17*, 261-267.

Hare, A. *Handbook of Small Group Research*. New York: The Free Press of Glencoe, 1962.

Hare, A. Theories of group development and categories for interaction analysis. *Small Group Behavior*, 1973, *4*, 259-304.

Harré, R. and Secord, P. *The Explanation of Social Behavior*.

Totowa, New Jersey: Littlefield, Adams and Co., 1973.

Harth, R. Changing attitudes toward school, classroom behavior, and reaction to frustration of emotionally disturbed children through role-playing. *Exceptional Children*, 1966, *33*, 119-120.

Hartup, W. Peer interaction and social organization. In P. Mussen (Ed.), *Carmichael's Manual of Child Psychology* (Vol. 2; 3rd edition). New York: John Wiley and Sons, 1970, 361-456.

Hassett, J. and Weisberg, A. *Open Education: Alternatives Within Our Tradition*. Englewood Cliffs, New Jersey: Prentice-Hall, 1972.

Heinkel, O. Evaluation of simulation as a teaching device. *Journal of Experimental Education*, 1970, *38*, 32-36.

Hemphill, J. Why people attempt to lead. In L. Petrullo and B. Bass (Eds.), *Leadership and Interpersonal Behavior*. New York: Holt, Rinehart, and Winston, 1961, 201-215.

Hendry, C., Lippitt, R., and Zander, A. *Reality Practice as Educational Method*. Psychodrama Monograph 9. New York: Beacon House, 1947.

Herbert, C. *Social Role and Linguistic Variation*. Unpublished doctoral dissertation, Claremont Graduate School, Claremont, California, 1970.

Herron, R. and Sutton-Smith, B. (Eds.) *Child's Play*. New York: John Wiley and Sons, 1971.

Hertzberg, A. and Stone, E. *Schools Are for Children*. New York: Schocken Publishing Co., 1971.

Hoetker, J. *Dramatics and the Teaching of Literature*. Champaign, Illinois: National Council of Teachers of English, 1969.

Homans, G. *The Human Group*. New York: Harcourt, Brace, and World, 1950.

Hudgins, B. Effects of group experience on individual problem solving. *Journal of Educational Psychology*, 1960, *51*, 37-42.

Hudgins, B. and Smith, L. Group structure and productivity in problem-solving. *Journal of Educational Psychology* 1966, *57*, 287-296.

Inbar, M. and Stoll, C. *Simulation and Gaming in Social Science.* New York: Free Press, 1972.

Institute for the Development of Educational Activities. *Learning in the Small Group.* Dayton, Ohio: Author, 1971.

Johnson, D. *The Social Psychology of Education.* New York: Holt, Rinehart, and Winston, 1970.

Johnson, D. *Reaching Out.* Englewood Cliffs, New Jersey: Prentice-Hall, Inc., 1972.

Johnson, D. and Johnson, F. *Joining Together.* Englewood Cliffs, New Jersey: Prentice-Hall, Inc., 1975.

Johnson, D. and Johnson, R. Instructional goal structure: Cooperative, competitive, or individualistic. *Review of Educational Research,* 1974, *44,* 213-240.

Kelley, H. and Thibaut, J. Group problem solving. In G. Lindzey and E. Aronson (Eds.), *The Handbook of Social Psychology,* (Vol. 4; 2nd edition). Reading, Massachusetts: Addison-Wesley, 1969.

Kiesler, C., and Kiesler, S. *Conformity.* Reading, Massachusetts: Addison-Wesley, 1970.

Klein, A. *How to Use Role-Playing Effectively.* New York: The Association Press, 1959.

Langer, J. Disequilibrium as a source of development. In P. Mussen, J. Langer, and M. Covington (Eds.), *Trends and Issues in Developmental Psychology.* New York: Holt, Rinehart, and Winston, 1969.

Laughlin, P. Selection strategies in concept attainment as a function of number of persons and stimulus display. *Journal of Experimental Psychology,* 1965, *5,* 115-119.

Laughlin, P. and Doherty, M. Discussion versus memory in cooperative group concept attainment. *Journal of Educational Psychology,* 1967, *58,* 123-128.

Laughlin, P., McGlynn, P., Anderson, J., and Jacobson, E. Concept attainment by individual versus cooperative pairs as a function of memory, sex, and concept rule. *Journal of*

Personality and Social Psychology, 1968, *8*, 410-417.

Levine, J. and Butler, J. Lecture versus group decision in changing behavior. *Journal of Applied Psychology*, 1952, *36*, 29-33.

Lewis, D. and Wentworth, D. *Games and Simulations for Teaching Economics*. New York: Joint Council on Economic Education, 1971.

Leypoldt, M. *Forty Ways to Teach in Groups*. Valley Forge, Pennsylvania: Judson Press, 1967.

Lin, N. *The Study of Human Communications*. Indianapolis: The Bobbs-Merrill Co., 1973.

Lippitt, R. and Gold, M. Classroom social structure as a mental health problem. *Journal of Social Issues*, 1959, *15*, 40-58.

Lippitt, R. and Hubbell, A. Role-playing for personnel and guidance workers. *Group Psychotherapy*, 1956, *9*, 89-114.

Livingston, S. and Stoll, C. *Simulation Games: An Introduction for the Social Studies Teacher*. New York: Free Press, 1973.

Lott, A. and Lott, B. Group cohesiveness, communication level, and conformity. *Journal of Abnormal and Social Psychology*, 1961, *62*, 408-412.

Lott, A. and Lott, B. Group cohesiveness and individual learning. *Journal of Educational Psychology*, 1966, *57*, 61-73.

Maccoby, E. Role-taking in childhood and its consequences for social learning. *Child Development*, 1959, *30*, 239-252.

Magers, J. The role-playing technique in teaching a novel. *English Journal*, 1968, *57*, 990-991.

Maier, N. and Solem, A. The contribution of a discussion leader to the quality of group thinking: The effective use of minority opinions. *Human Relations*, 1952, *5*, 277-288.

Mann, J. Experimental evaluations of role playing. *Psychological Bulletin*, 1956, *53*, 227-234.

McKeachie, W. Individual conformity to attitudes of classroom groups. *Journal of Abnormal and Social Psychology*, 1954, *49*, 282-289.

Meehan, M. and Schusler, R. Small groups in sixth grade. *The*

Elementary School Journal, 1966, *67,* 241-245.

Miel, A. *Cooperative Procedures in Learning.* New York: Teachers College, Columbia University, 1952.

Moreno, J. *Psychodrama.* New York: Beacon House, 1946.

Moreno, J. *Who Shall Survive* (Rev. edition). New York: Beacon House, 1953.

Murray, F. Acquisitions of conservation through social interaction. *Developmental Psychology,* 1972, *6,* 1-6.

Napier, R. and Gershenfeld, M. *Groups: Theory and Experience.* Boston: Houghton Mifflin Co., 1973.

Nesbitt, W. *Simulation Games for the Social Studies Classroom.* Foreign Policy Association, 1971.

Nichols, H. and Williams, L. *Learning About Role-Playing for Children and Teachers.* Washington, D.C.: Association for Childhood Education International, 1960.

Olson, M. Ways to achieve quality in school classrooms: Some definitive answers. *Phi Delta Kappan,* 1971, September, 63-65.

Perry, H. The living newspaper. *English Journal,* 1950, *39,* 11-15.

Piaget, J. *The Language and Thought of the Child.* London: Routledge and Kegan Paul, 1926.

Piaget, J. *The Moral Judgment of the Child.* New York: Harcourt, Brace, and World, 1932.

Piaget, J. *Play, Dreams, and Imitation in Childhood.* New York: W.W. Norton, 1951.

Piaget, J. *Science of Education and the Psychology of the Child.* New York: Orion Press, 1970.

Piaget, J. and Inhelder, B. *The Psychology of the Child.* New York: Basic Books, 1969.

Pope, B. Socioeconomic contrasts in children's peer culture prestige values. *Genetic Psychology Monographs,* 1953, *48,* 319-348.

Rehage, K. A comparison of pupil-teacher planning and teacher-directed procedures in eighth grade social studies classes.

Journal of Educational Research, 1951, *45*, 111-115.

Reissman, F. *The Culturally Deprived Child*. New York: Harper and Brothers, 1962.

Rogers, V. *Teaching in the British Primary School*. New York: Macmillan Co., 1970.

Rubin, L. (Ed.) *Improving In-Service Education*. Boston: Allyn and Bacon, Inc., 1971.

Sarason, S. *The Culture of the School and the Problem of Change*. Boston: Allyn and Bacon, Inc., 1971.

Sarbin, T., and Allen, V. Role theory. In G. Lindzey and E. Aronson (Eds.), *Handbook of Social Psychology* (Vol. 1; 2nd edition). Reading, Massachusetts: Addison-Wesley, 1968, 488-567.

Sayre, W. Role participation and the teacher of anthropology. *Journal of General Education*, 1957, *10*, 108-113.

Scheidel, T. and Crowell, L. Idea development in small discussion groups. *The Quarterly Journal of Speech*, 1964, *50*, 140-145.

Schmuck, R. Some relationships of peer liking patterns in the classroom to pupil attitudes and achievement. *School Review*, 1963, *3*, 59-65.

Schmuck, R. Some aspects of classroom social climate. *Psychology in the Schools*, 1966, *3*, 59-65.

Schmuck, R. and Miles, M. *Organization Development in Schools*. Palo Alto, California: National Press Books, 1971.

Schmuck, R. and Runkel, P. *Handbook of Organization Development in Schools*. Palo Alto, California: National Press Books, 1972.

Schmuck, R. and Schmuck, P. *Group Processes in the Classroom*. Dubuque, Iowa: William C. Brown, Co., 1971.

Schmuck, R. and Schmuck, P. *A Humanistic Psychology of Education*. Palo Alto, California: National Press Books, 1974.

Schutz, W. *FIRO: A Three-Dimensional Theory of Interpersonal Behavior*. New York: Holt, Rinehart, and Winston, 1958.

Shaftel, G. and Shaftel, F. *Role-Playing the Problem Story*. New

York: National Conference of Christians and Jews, 1952.

Shaftel, F. and Shaftel, G. *Role-Playing for Social Values.* Englewood Cliffs, New Jersey: Prentice-Hall, 1967.

Sharan, S. and Colodner, C. Counselor: A simulation game for vocational decision-making. School of Education, Tel-Aviv University, 1975.

Shaw, M. *Group Dynamics: The Psychology of Small Group Behavior.* New York: McGraw-Hill, 1971.

Shaw, M. and Shaw, L. Some effects of sociometric grouping upon learning in a second grade classroom. *Journal of Social Psychology*, 1962, *57*, 453-458.

Sherif, M. *The Psychology of Group Norms.* New York: Harper and Row, 1936.

Shirts, G. Notes on defining "simulation." *Occasional Newsletter About Simulations and Games.* La Jolla, California: Western Behavioral Science Institute, 1972, *15*, 14-23.

Silberman, C. *Crisis in the Classroom.* New York: Random House, 1970.

Smedslund, J. Les origines sociales de la decentration. In F. Bresson and M. de Montmollin (Eds.), *Psychologie et Epistemologie Genetiques: Themes Piagetian.* Paris: Dunod, 1966.

Smith, H. *Sensitivity to People.* New York: McGraw-Hill, 1966.

Solomon, D. and Oberlander, M. Locus of control in the classroom. In R. Coop and K. White (Eds.), *Psychological Concepts in the Classroom.* New York: Harper and Row, 1974, 119-150.

Sommer, R. Classroom ecology. *Journal of Applied Behavioral Science*, 1967, *3*, 489-503.

Stanford, G. and Roark, A. *Human Interaction in Education.* Boston: Allyn and Bacon, 1974.

Stanford, G. and Stanford, B. *Learning Discussion Skills Through Games.* New York: Citation Press, 1969.

Steiner, I. *Group Process and Productivity.* New York: Academic Press, 1972.

Stephens, L. *The Teacher's Guide to Open Education*. New York: Holt, Rinehart, and Winston, 1974.

Stodgill, R. *Individual Behavior and Group Achievement*. New York: Oxford University Press, 1959.

Tanner, L. and Lindgren, H. *Classroom Teaching and Learning: A Mental Health Approach*. New York: Holt, Rinehart, and Winston, 1971.

Taylor, D. and Faust, W. Twenty questions: Efficiency in problem solving as a function of size of group. *Journal of Experimental Psychology*, 1952, *44*, 360-368.

Taylor, J. and Walford, R. *Simulation in the Classroom*. Middlesex, England: Penguin Books, 1972.

Thelen, H. Principle of least group size. *The School Review*, 1949, *57*, 139-148.

Thelen, H. *Dynamics of Groups at Work*. Chicago: University of Chicago Press, 1954.

Tuckman, B. Developmental sequence in small groups. *Psychological Bulletin*, 1965, *63*, 384-399.

Twelker, P. A Basic Reference Shelf on Simulation and Gaming. ERIC: ED 041-487, 1970.

Veatch, J. *Reading in the Elementary School*. New York: Ronald Press, 1966.

Voight, R. *Invitation to Learning: The Learning Center Handbook*. Washington, D.C.: Acropolis Books, 1971.

Wagner, G. and Hosier, M. *Reading Games*. New York: Teachers Publishing Corporation, 1960.

Weber, L. *The English Infant School and Informal Education*. Englewood Cliffs, New Jersey: Prentice-Hall, 1971.

White, K. and Howard, J. The relationship of achievement responsibility to instructional treatments. *The Journal of Experimental Education*, 1970, *39*, 78-82.

Wickens, D. Piagetian theory as a model for open systems of education. In M. Schwebel and J. Raph (Eds.), *Piaget in the Classroom*. New York: Basic Books, 1973, 179-198.

Wood, M. Role-playing: Effective in family relationship units. *Clearing House*, 1970, *26*, 469-471.

Zuckerman, D. and Horn, R. *The Guide to Simulations/Games for Education and Training*. Cambridge, Massachusetts: Information Resources, 1973.

Index

A

Achievement tests, 11, 12

B

Belonging, sense of, 44, 45
  see Group

C

Chairman
  role of, 38, 39-41
  see Group
Communication
  between group members, 22
  in Centers, 127
  clarifying, 111-113
  effect on small groups, 8
  in role playing, 159,
    162-163
Cooperation
  in Centers, 127
  and cohesiveness, 25-26
  in planning, 9
  in role playing, 159
  see Planning

Coordination, problems of,
    18-19
Curriculum, 5
  and role playing, 166

D

Dewey, John, 3, 4, 5, 27
  stages of logical thinking,
    101
Discussion
  arriving at a solution of,
    100-103
  clarifying topic of, 98
  emotion and logic in, 113
  formulating topic of,
    98-101
  leading, 105-106
  preparing for, 103-105

E

Environment, social, 4
Evaluation
  of Activity Centers,
    139-140

of contributions, 109-110
criteria of, 116
of group activity, 70-71
in higher grades, 116-118
of individuals and chairman,
  120-121
of information, 104-105
in lower grades, 115-116
of role playing, 176-177,
  178
of simulation games,
  195-197, 211
Expression, verbal, 13
of differing opinions, 98

G

Games
  distribution of speaking
    privileges, 111-113
  to encourage listening, 113
  example of simulation,
    189-191
  non-simulation learning,
    187
  small groups, 55-56
  "Thirty Questions," 56-57
Group
  assigned opinions, 50-52
  assigned roles, 48-50
  cohesiveness, 24-26, 29
  composing, 35-36
  equal roles, 48
  friendship patterns of,
    22-24

functioning, failures in,
  41-43
goals, definition of, 44-45
norms of, 26-28
size of, 30-32
social effects of, 7
spatial placement of mem-
  bers, 32
tasks for, 32-35
time schedules for, 36-37
Grouping, ability, 6

H

Helping, 69-70

I

Instructions, reading and understanding, 67-68
Interaction, problems of, 17
  patterns of, 29
Interviewing, 93-94
Intellectual development, 12,
  13-14

L

Leadership, 38-39
Learning Centers
  bulletin board as, 151-152
  cards for, 151
  diagnostic, 146-147
  enrichment, 145-146
  file as, 151
  independent learning,
    147-148

instructions for, 149
motivation in design of, 148
prescriptive, 147
project, 144-145
specific learning goals of, 148-149
work sheets for, 150
see Skills
Literature, and role playing, 167-168

M

Materials
in Activity Centers, 137
distributing, 68-69
to stimulate writing, 132-133
Mathematics, in Activity Centers, 134-135
Motivation
see Learning Centers; Simulation Games

O

Observer, role of, 119
Observation feedback exercise, 121
schedules, 122-124
Organization, and small group teaching, 6
problems, 18

P

Piaget, Jean, 3, 4, 5, 13

and role playing, 161-162, 165
Planning
cooperative, of units, 78-81, 81-84
preliminary, 34-35
procedures, 45
of simulation game, 201-205
time factor in, 79
Problem-solving, 11, 15
in role playing, 166

Q

Questionnaires and rating scales, 121-122

R

Reading, in Activity Centers, 133-134, 138
in diagnostic center, 146-147
Record-keeping, in Activity Centers, 139
Research, and group norms, 27
Responsibility
in discussion, 103
for experiences, 9
for research, 34
for studies, in open classroom, 131
Role playing
choosing actors, 172-173, 183

determining background materials, 173, 184
discussion of, 176, 185
possible topics, 166-169
re-enactment, 177-178, 185
selecting topic, 170-172, 183
session, 174-176
training audience, 173-174, 184
see Curriculum; Evaluation; Teacher
Role taking, 161
affective-social approach to, 163-164
cognitive-communications approach to, 162-163
social-learning approach to, 164-165

S
Simulation Games
building model of relationships for, 206-207
choosing roles and players for, 207
choosing topics and goals for, 205-206
formulating rules for, 209-210
motivation in, 192-195
scheduling events of, 210
and small-group teaching, 191-192

and studying complex processes, 197-198
see Evaluation; Planning
Skills
centers for improving, 141-144
identifying, 130-131
learning, 87-88
participation, 114-115
Social context for learning, 4, 8, 11
Social status, 23

T
Teacher, 33, 42, 59
in Activity Centers, 138-139
as advisor and guide, 130-131
guiding role play, 178-180
role of, 4, 10, 128
Thought, abstract, 12

U
Unit, dividing into sub-topics, 84-87
see Planning; Learning Centers

W
Writing, in Activity Centers, 132-133
see Materials

About the Authors

SHLOMO SHARAN, formerly Sheldon Singer, is a native of Milwaukee, Wisconsin. He received his Ph.D. degree in Clinical Psychology from Yeshiva University, New York, and served for several years as staff psychologist, Department of Psychiatry, Albert Einstein College of Medicine and the Bronx Municipal Hospital Center. Since 1966 he has been teaching at Tel-Aviv University in Israel, where his interests have turned to social-psychological issues in education. He also serves as a consultant to Israel Educational Television for a series of teacher-training programs on small-group teaching, and is engaged in research on that topic and on ethnic interaction and integration in the schools.

YAEL SHARAN was born in Tel-Aviv. She holds a B.A. degree in Special Education from the Hebrew University in Jerusalem and an M.A. degree in Remedial Reading from City College of the City University of New York. She has taught in elementary schools in Israel and the United States. Since 1969 she has been involved in training teachers at the Kibbutz Teachers College, Tel-Aviv. She has a private practice in remedial reading, and serves as a consultant on small-group teaching to the Elementary Science Teaching Project at the School of Education, Tel-Aviv University.

Small-Group Teaching is the second book which the Sharans have written together. An earlier volume, entitled *The Psychology and Remediation of Learning Disabilities* (in Hebrew), was published by Sifriat Poalim, Tel-Aviv.